Because I Feel Fat

Because I Feel Fat

◆

Helping the Ones You Love Deal with an Eating Disorder

Tony Paulson, Ph.D.
Johanna Marie McShane, Ph.D.

iUniverse, Inc.
New York Lincoln Shanghai

Because I Feel Fat
Helping the Ones You Love Deal with an Eating Disorder

iUniverse, Inc.

For information address:
iUniverse, Inc.
2021 Pine Lake Road, Suite 100
Lincoln, NE 68512
www.iuniverse.com

ISBN: 0-595-32061-9

Printed in the United States of America

Contents

Preface

How We Came To Write *Because I Feel Fat...*

Because I Feel Fat... is the result of years of treating people with eating disorders and seeing the fear, frustration, anger, and confusion family and friends experience as they witness the extreme, self-destructive behavior that most often accompanies anorexia and bulimia nervosa. We have been asked many times by family and friends of people with these disorders to help them understand why their loved ones behave the way they do. Often times they want to help but do not know what to do. Instead, they feel helpless and frustrated as they watch their loved ones become increasingly consumed by their eating disorders.

Our primary goal in writing *Because I Feel Fat...* is to describe eating disorders "from the inside out." To do this we have asked women suffering from anorexia and bulimia to share their stories and to give us an inside view of what it is like to live with an eating disorder. These women describe their experiences of being consumed by a compelling yet destructive thought process, and of trying to deal with the intense fears that are part of eating disorders.

We hope that by providing this inside view of what it is like to have an eating disorder, family and friends will feel less helpless and have more patience and compassion throughout their loved one's recovery process. In addition, having a better understanding of eating disorders can assist in making more informed treatment decisions, which can lead to more effective treatment outcomes.

Introduction

o o o o o o o o o o o o o o o o o o o o o o o o o o o o o o o o

*"I'm watching her die. She is just fading away and there's nothing I
can do about it."*

—*Comments from the father of a 17-year-old with anorexia*

At least 5 to 10 million girls and women in the United States suffer from
anorexia and bulimia. Eating disorders are dangerous and destructive psy-
chological/biological conditions that profoundly affect people's lives.
These ailments, in fact, have one of the highest death rates of any psychological disorder; up to 15% of people die as a direct result of their disorder,
and the likelihood of death increases with the length of time a person has
the disorder. Early detection and treatment, therefore, are crucial. Unfortunately, eating disorders are often associated with a great deal of shame,
embarrassment, guilt and confusion that get in the way of someone pursuing the treatment she needs.

What makes eating disorders especially frustrating is that they are
extremely complicated, and there is no clear consensus about what actually
causes them. We suspect that a combination of psychological, interper-
sonal, social, and biological factors are at play. We are uncertain, however,
as to exactly how these conditions interact to create and maintain an eating
disorder.

We do know that anorexia and bulimia are highly destructive disorders
that greatly affect not only the person directly suffering from the disorder,
but also her family and friends. From the perspective of family and friends,
eating disorders are perplexing, frustrating, and seem to make no sense

whatsoever. Family and friends often feel helpless as they watch their loved one slowly destroy herself.

To the person with an eating disorder, her behavior makes a lot of sense, and she is often confused about why others have such difficulties understanding. For instance, she feels overweight, so it seems obvious to her to restrict her food intake. Or she believes "what I just ate will make me fat," so she purges to get rid it. For her, it is a simple process of avoiding weight gain or getting fat.

The intent of this book is to help you understand why your loved one does what she does. We do this by presenting eating disorders from the perspective of people who suffer from them. Throughout the book, we take you into their world to share with you what anorexia and bulimia mean to them and how they live day to day, moment to moment—consumed with thoughts of fat, calories, body size, and weight. We hope that with more insight into what your loved one is experiencing, your feelings of helplessness and frustration will decrease and your understanding of what you can do to help her will be more clear.

Journey Into The World Of Eating Disorders

The book is divided into three sections. We begin our journey into the world of eating disorders with an introduction to anorexia and bulimia. Here, we discuss the most common signs and symptoms found in each of these disorders and present typical medical complications associated with them. A discussion of some causes of eating disorders concludes this first section.

In the second section, our journey continues by focusing in detail on the subjective experiences of those who suffer with eating disorders. This section will help you—as a father, mother, brother, sister, spouse, friend, or other loved one—understand what an eating disorder is like from the perspective of the person living with it.

The final section of *Because I Feel Fat...* deals with what to do when you discover that your loved one has an eating disorder. Finding the right treatment is essential, but getting help can be a confusing and frustrating process that often leaves people feeling helpless and without a clear direction. We discuss options for treatment and describe what to expect as your loved one recovers from her disorder.

Their Words

Our guides for this journey are women who are suffering from eating disorders. We invited them to tell us their stories, and they did. They courageously constructed a window for us to look into their lives and into eating disorders. Their openness and willingness to share their stories have created a unique opportunity for you to see the world through their eyes.

PART I
See Their World

1

Bingeing, Purging, Starving:
What's the Difference?
The Basics of Eating Disorders

Anorexia Nervosa

An intense fear of being overweight drives people with anorexia nervosa. For them, "being fat" is terrifying and threatening. They see weight and body size as something they should have complete control over, and they regard not being "thin enough" as a sign of weakness and failure.

For someone with anorexia, the fear of weight gain is so acute that she will go to extraordinary lengths to be thin. A 23-year-old woman with anorexia illustrated this extreme fear when she told us,

> *I would rather be dead than fat.*

Not surprisingly, a central feature of anorexia is weight loss. The drop in weight can happen suddenly and rapidly or gradually over time, but when left unchecked, it can become extreme. Restricting food intake or fasting altogether and exercising excessively are the most common behaviors in anorexia. In addition, some women with anorexia purge what they eat via self-induced vomiting, or they use laxatives or diuretics to maintain their low weight. A 27-year-old with anorexia remarked,

> *I get rid of just about everything. It really depends on the type of day I'm having. I mean, sometimes I'll get rid of a cup of coffee.*

Another woman stated,

> *If I feel it in my stomach, I'm getting rid of it. It doesn't matter what it is, I'm getting rid of it...I can't stand to feel anything in my stomach.*

Characteristics of Anorexia

Anorexia may begin as a diet and sometimes even seems relatively harmless at first. Although the person may start out feeling she is in control of her behaviors, the disorder eventually controls her and begins to erode her life. Anorexia, like other eating disorders, is so powerful and sneaky that often she does not realize that the disorder is beginning to control her, instead of her controlling the disorder.

Generally, a woman with anorexia fiercely protects and passionately defends her behavior. In the early stages of the disease, she usually feels in control and quite invincible. She very much does not want to change or give up the disorder, and she will fight ferociously to keep anyone from getting in the way of her anorexic behaviors. As the disease progresses, however, the sense of power and control begins to erode, and she may start to feel hopeless, helpless, and out of control. Frequently, even when she feels out of control and believes that the disease has taken over her life, she is so dependent on restricting food and losing weight and so afraid of what will happen if she changes her behavior that she continues to fight to keep the disorder.

Ritualistic behaviors regarding food are common in anorexia. Persons with this disorder often are frantic about which foods they eat. In addition, calories are rigorously counted and tracked, and food may be eaten in very specific ways. One 18-year-old talks about what she does to make food seem safe enough for her to eat.

> *I have to cut up anything I eat into an even number of pieces—usually 20 or 30. It is better if the number of pieces can be divided by 5; that makes it easier to eat. If the food is not cut like this, I can't eat it.*

The specific warning signs of anorexia include:

Bingeing, Purging, Starving: What's the Difference? The Basics of Eating   5

Disorders

- Preoccupation with weight
- Persistent drive to be thin
- Withdrawal from friends
- Preoccupation with food
- Irritability or mood swings
- Fear of particular foods
- Compulsive counting of calories or fat
- Intense fear of gaining weight
- Compulsive exercising
- Weight loss
- Lying about eating
- Concern about how food is prepared
- Low self-esteem
- Depression (can include suicidal thoughts or attempts)
- Feelings of hopelessness
- Intense sensitivity to criticism
- Difficulty identifying physical or emotional feelings (feels out of touch with feelings)
- Frequently weighing oneself
- Dissatisfaction with body size and shape
- Irregular menstrual cycle or cessation of menstruation (amenorrhea)
- Perfectionist standards; high achievement expectations
- Difficulty concentrating or thinking
- Denial about illness or about severity of illness
- Being overly concerned with what others think
- Growth of fine hair (called lanugo) on arms, face, or back

- Rigid thoughts or behaviors (rituals with food, compulsive schedule-making)
- Intense fear of failure

This is not an exhaustive list, and it is important to remember that any one symptom alone does not mean someone has an eating disorder.

Medical Complications of Anorexia Nervosa

Eating disorders carry serious, potentially fatal medical complications. An estimated 10% to 15% of individuals suffering from these disorders will die as a direct result of them These are the most common medical consequences of anorexia:

- Weakening of the heart due to malnutrition (including potential heart failure)
- Low blood pressure
- Low body temperature
- Irregularities in, or loss of, menstruation
- Dehydration
- Electrolyte imbalance (essential minerals found in the blood)
- Anemia
- Gastrointestinal disturbances
- Osteoporosis
- Lowered immune system function/low resistance to infection
- Hypoglycemia
- Kidney impairment

Being Thin Versus Feeling Thin

One of the perplexing characteristics of anorexia is that the person with the disorder does not feel or see herself as thin, no matter what her actual weight. People often wonder how someone can possibly look in the mirror and not comprehend that she is underweight. What happens is that anorexia distorts the person's perception, so she cannot see herself accurately. This distortion affects each individual differently. For example, some people with anorexia see themselves as overweight, no matter what the reality; others see themselves as too thin in some ways, but feel that certain parts of their bodies are out of proportion or fat.

One 21-year-old with anorexia told us,

My arms are thin. Probably too thin. But my legs, my legs, and especially my butt. If you could see my legs and butt, you'd see what I was talking about.

An 18-year-old said,

I'm just huge. There isn't a part of me that isn't fat and disgusting. I'm an embarrassment.

For the person with anorexia, it's not about whether or not anyone else thinks she is thin. Instead, it is about whether *she* experiences herself as thin. Whether she experiences herself as thin often has to do with how she feels at a particular moment, and how she feels at that moment can be based on many things. For example, whether people seemed to like her that day, how well or poorly she did on a test at school, or what she ate or did not eat during the day can all affect how she perceives her weight and body. So, even though you see her as being dangerously thin, she does not experience herself that way. She may concede that parts of her are thin, but overall she does not perceive herself as too thin.

A 26-year-old woman described the discrepancy between how she sees herself and how others see her.

I know other people look at me and see me as thin, but I don't. I don't feel thin. Its about how I feel.... It's hard to explain, but sometimes I feel thin, but most of the time I don't.... My clothes don't fit like I want them or I feel my stomach sticking out.... I feel fat!

Because of the distortion anorexia creates, satisfaction with any weight loss is short lived. As soon as the person loses weight, she quickly begins to feel "not thin" at this new body size, and she must pursue further weight loss.

As she continues to lose weight, someone with anorexia may experience a sense of pride or strength because of her ability to deprive herself of food. She may also experience a feeling of power because she can withstand hunger and other people's attempts to make her eat. As a 21-year-old put it,

> *I remember walking into the cafeteria and looking at everyone eating lunch and thinking that I was somehow better than them. I mean, I was able to do something they weren't. Not eat.*

Bulimia Nervosa

Bulimia nervosa is characterized by episodes of binge eating, followed by behavior designed to get rid of what was just eaten.

The Binge

A binge used to be thought of as the consumption of large amounts of food. Clinicians now realize that the term "bingeing" can mean different things to different people. In general, bingeing is defined as eating, in a discrete period of time, an amount of food that is larger than most people would eat under similar circumstances. What constitutes a binge, however, depends primarily on the perspective of the person who is doing the eating. For example, for one person a binge might be eating a typical full meal, whereas another person may feel she has binged after eating a single piece of bread. Still others consider bingeing as consuming far larger quantities of food than one would find in a typical meal. A 30-year-old with bulimia described what bingeing means to her.

> *Sometimes I can drink a glass of water and feel like I have binged. Then I have to go and throw it up.*

Another woman with the disorder said,

> *I plan my binge all day. Then I go to the store and buy as much food as I can. I will buy gallons of ice cream, bags of cookies, and anything else I see. I eat until I am in so much pain that I can't eat any more. Then I can purge.*

The Purge

After someone has binged, she experiences a dramatic need to get rid of the food. Typically, she will use self-induced vomiting, laxatives, diuretics (water pills), emetics (such as syrup of ipecac), or excessive exercise to accomplish this. How often someone binges and purges varies greatly, and the frequency can change over time or according to circumstances. In addition to purging, someone with bulimia may also engage in dieting or fasting as a way of preventing weight gain.

Although someone with bulimia can be as preoccupied with food, weight, fat, and calories as someone with anorexia, she does not usually suffer from the dramatic weight losses seen in anorexia. People with bulimia are more often than not at a relatively normal body weight, but they can also be slightly underweight or overweight. In cases where the person is underweight and purges, she is at increased risk of medical complications. Purging is taxing for anyone's body, but it is particularly dangerous when someone is below her normal weight.

The specific warning signs for bulimia include:

- Bingeing
- Impulsive behavior (stealing, lying, risky behaviors)
- Hoarding or stealing food
- Use of laxatives, diuretics (water pills), emetics (such as ipecac), diet pills
- Secretive eating
- Water retention

- Swollen glands
- Frequent trips to the bathroom, especially directly after eating
- Low self-esteem
- Feelings of hopelessness
- Intense sensitivity to criticism
- Eating when not physically hungry
- Feelings of disgust or self-hatred
- Obsessive or compulsive behavior ·
- Difficulty identifying physical and emotional feelings (feels out of touch with feelings)
- Overly concerned with what others think
- Excessive exercise
- Often wants to stop behavior, but does not know how to
- Perfectionist standards; high achievement expectations
- Depression (can include suicidal thoughts or attempts)
- Irritability or mood swings
- Feelings of shame, guilt, embarrassment, or humiliation about eating behavior
- Dissatisfaction with body size and shape
- Change in social behavior (often withdrawal or isolation)
- Feeling out of control (with regard to eating or other aspects of life)
- Weight fluctuations

Medical Complications of Bulimia

Fewer people die from bulimia than from anorexia, and because of this, the physical impact of this eating disorder is often ignored or minimized. Despite the lower death rate, people with bulimia, nevertheless, can end up with serious and even life-threatening medical problems. Common medical complications seen in bulimia include:

- Electrolyte imbalance (essential minerals found in blood)

- Menstrual irregularities

- Potential heart arrhythmia or irregularities (due to electrolyte imbalances)

- Esophageal bleeding or rupture

- Gastrointestinal dysfunction (such as ulceration, abdominal pain, bleeding, bloating, constipation, non-responsive bowels)

- Tooth decay

2

Why Did This Happen?
Causes of Eating Disorders

Although the past two decades have seen an enormous amount of research having to do with eating disorders, there is no clear consensus about exactly how these disorders develop. Some common explanations revolve around society's preoccupation with thinness. The drive to be thin no doubt plays a part in how anorexia and bulimia develop, although it is not the only contributing factor. Psychological, social, familial, and perhaps biological factors also play a part in how and why an eating disorder develops.

You Can Never Be Too Rich Or Too Thin

Both women and men in our culture face pressure to look a certain way. Women, nevertheless, face more intense pressure in this area, particularly when it comes to being thin.

A thinner, less-rounded body shape as the "ideal body" has replaced the once-admired hourglass figure that was popular in the early and middle part of the twentieth century. This trend toward thinness became evident in the 1960s when a British model nicknamed Twiggy burst onto the American modeling scene. She was 17 years old, and at 5'7", she weighed only 97 pounds. With measurements of 31-22-32, she quickly captured the fashion scene. It was not long before many girls and women began patterning their makeup, hair, clothing, and body shape after hers.

In western society, thinness is associated with personal and professional success, with wealth, and with strength and power. In addition, some people believe that if they can just become thin enough, life's problems will somehow magically disappear.

Conversely, our society devalues any body shape considered overweight. Individuals who are overweight are viewed as weak and less intelligent, thus they are less often chosen for some types of jobs and are thought less capable of being social and having relationships of various kinds. They are also stereotyped as lonely, shy, greedy for affection, and overly dependent on others. These attitudes usually start early in childhood. A 25-year-old with anorexia remembers her elementary school years,

> *I was very overweight and I got teased. I was so lonely and always felt left out. No one wanted to be my friend. I decided early on that I had better not stay fat.*

No matter what they do, most women will never reach the level of thinness portrayed as ideal in our society. Subsequently, they will spend their lives feeling inadequate and dissatisfied with themselves.

Because societal and cultural pressures are so powerful and so pervasive, it may seem surprising that more people do not have eating disorders. But for someone to develop anorexia or bulimia, other factors must be present in addition to those of culture and society.

Psychological And Personality Characteristics

Possible psychological factors that contribute to eating-disordered behaviors are wide ranging. For example, eating-disordered behaviors can be conceptualized as attempts by passive, dependent individuals to exert control over their environments. From this perspective, fear of fatness is a reflection of fear of losing control. Because loss of control may occur with eating, food is viewed as dangerous, and is thus avoided. By successfully restricting food, your loved one begins to feel a sense of mastery over her life.

With respect to bulimia, the sense of mastery is lost with the consumption of food and all the negative qualities associated with it, including a perceived loss of personal control and the potential for weight gain. A sense of mastery is regained by ridding oneself of the ingested food. The binge/purge cycle provides the bulimic a temporary sense of well-being, mastery, relief from distressing emotions, and a sense of comfort.

Women with eating disorders also tend to believe that life is very unpredictable, uncertain, and dangerous. To make things even more frightening for them, these women often don't feel that they are very powerful, or they think that they don't have the right to use the power they do have.

Limiting or restricting food intake and the weight loss that results can make someone feel as if she is in control of herself and her life, and it can also make her feel tremendously powerful. An 18-year-old with anorexia put it this way,

> My life has always felt so chaotic. I never knew what was going to happen next, and that was really scary. My eating and my weight are something I know I can control. No matter what, I can always count on my eating disorder.

Another person with anorexia who is 25 years old said,

> If I don't eat, I feel so in control and powerful. I feel like there is nothing I can't do. But if I eat anything, even one grape, it all comes crashing down and I feel weak and helpless and like I am a failure.

Finally, a 19-year-old with bulimia shared,

> I can't control anything in my life, ever. But I can control my bingeing and purging. No one can stop me from doing it.

It has also been suggested that people with certain types of personalities may be predisposed to developing an eating disorder. Characteristics such as perfectionism or being highly driven, high achieving, or extremely ambitious are typically found in people with anorexia and bulimia.

Biology

Many people who suffer from anorexia or bulimia also suffer from depression. It has been suggested that the same chemicals in our brain that contribute to depression may also play a role in eating disorders. Individuals who have eating disorders may have imbalances in chemicals called "neurotransmitters," which play a part in both mood regulation and appetite.

Disturbances in amounts of the neurotransmitter Serotonin might contribute to depression and to the impulsive behavior toward food that people with bulimia experience. Furthermore, those with anorexia have been found to have lower levels of another neurotransmitter, Norepinephrine, which is believed to be partly responsible for regulating mood, alertness, and reactions to stress. Imbalances in Norepinephrine could answer some important questions about anorexia, such as why people with this disorder have such an acute ability to refuse food even though they are hungry, and why anorexia and other eating-disordered behaviors often increase in times of stress.

One of the difficulties in deciphering a biological component in eating disorders is determining whether an imbalance in neurotransmitters precipitates the development of an eating disorder or whether the imbalance occurs as a result of having an eating disorder. Another problem is figuring out exactly how and in what ways these chemicals might be affecting eating disorders.

Biology likely plays an important role in developing and maintaining anorexia and bulimia. Unfortunately, at this time our understanding of biology's role is limited. It is anticipated that as research in this area continues we will identify more clearly the specific biological factors that contribute to eating disorders.

The Family

Significant attention has been paid to the family dynamics of people with eating disorders. Unfortunately, trying to understand how family relationships may influence the development of an eating disorder sometimes leads to blaming families or particular family members. To do so is neither helpful nor accurate. Our experience has been that families, in general, try to do the very best they can.

Ascertaining and understanding how family interactions and patterns may affect anorexia and bulimia can benefit both the person with the disorder and her family. Recovery from an eating disorder in many ways involves the whole family—not just the person with the disorder.

Struggling With Emotions

Eating disorders tend to show up in families that have difficulties with emotions. Perhaps, for varying reasons, these families seem to have trouble acknowledging and expressing their emotions and tolerating or dealing with their feelings.

In some families, members may try to avoid feelings or even pretend that emotions don't exist. They may believe that certain emotions are bad or unacceptable, and that those feelings should never be seen or perhaps even felt. A 35-year-old woman with bulimia said,

> *In my family you always had to act pretty. You could never be mad or loud—you could never make noise. I learned to not show what I was really feeling. Sometimes I'm still not even sure what I'm feeling.*

In other families, emotions may be expressed but some family members may not feel safe with how other members handle their feelings. For instance, a 30-year-old with bulimia said of her childhood,

> *My father was really volatile. He could get really mad and yell. I hated it. It felt so unsafe and out of control. I hate that I could have feelings in me that might be scary and out of control.*

A common theme in eating disorders is confusion about what emotions mean and how someone is supposed to handle her feelings. The women who spoke to us recalled having difficulty understanding and knowing what to do with emotions in their families. A-29-year old with anorexia told us,

> *I never knew what my mom was up to. When I came home from school, she could be in any kind of mood. It was so unpredictable. Sometimes she would be depressed, other times she would be angry for no apparent reason, and sometimes she would be happy. It just seemed so unpredictable and dangerous. I tried everything I could think of to make her happy. Finally, I figured that if I always acted happy it might make her happy also. I'm not sure if that ever really worked, but at least it gave me something to do—something I could try.*

They Grow Up So Fast

In addition to difficulties with emotions, families where an eating disorder is present often have difficulty with changes, transitions, and maneuvering through the stages of children's development. Adapting to the shifting relationships and developmental stages that are part of the process of growing up and becoming an adult can certainly be challenging.

Sometimes parents have trouble giving their daughter who has an eating disorder more independence or responsibility. These parents may worry that something might happen to their daughter or that they are not being responsible parents by allowing her to take chances or risk making mistakes. One 18-year-old with bulimia said this about her relationship with her parents:

> *They worry so much—especially my mom. It's not like I'm doing anything irresponsible or dangerous, but they totally don't trust me. How do they think I'm going to learn to take care of myself unless they let me make my own choices? If they keep making decisions for me all the time, its never going to work. Anyway, I'll just rebel against them.*

PART II
Listen to Their Words

3

It's Really About...

Information about signs and symptoms of eating disorders is essential for friends and family to be able to recognize whether their loved one has an eating disorder. At the same time, though, this information is just part of the picture. To really help those who suffer from anorexia or bulimia, you need to understand how they experience themselves and their disorder.

Even family and friends who know the warning signs of an eating disorder and appreciate what their loved one says about her experience of living with the disorder may still have difficulty understanding why she is so attached to her eating disorder and why the disorder makes so much sense to her. Her behavior is so clearly dangerous and harmful, and the distress that the eating disorder causes is so great, that it's hard to imagine how anyone could find these behaviors beneficial.

Family and friends of those with eating disorders often believe that eating disorders happen because someone wants to be thin or is trying to be "extra healthy" or "more attractive." We have often heard individuals with anorexia or bulimia say that their disorder is related only to food, weight, and thinness. When we look and listen closely, however, we can see that there is much more to the picture than calories, fat, and an obsession with being thin.

Sometimes families and friends of people with eating disorders feel as if their loved one is deliberately trying to injure or kill herself. Certainly, the behavior involved in a serious eating disorder can be quite damaging, even life threatening. It is not surprising that someone might conclude that the person is setting out to destroy herself. As the mother of a 22-year-old with anorexia lamented,

She's just slowly killing herself. Doesn't she know that?

Dealing With Life

A paradox is at work here, however, and it may seem surprising at first glance. Understanding how the paradox works is important because it illustrates, in part, why the person with the eating disorder does not view her symptoms as dangerous. It also helps explain why she can have such a difficult time giving up the disorder.

The truth is, a person with anorexia or bulimia perceives herself to be continually in danger. She feels she is constantly about to be overwhelmed. Ironically, her eating disorder, which is actually destroying her, is experienced by her as a source of support. Your loved one does not feel threatened by her eating disorder. To the contrary, she feels more threatened *without* her eating disorder. Over time, the eating disorder becomes an indispensable relationship, one that she relies on to help her navigate through life. A helpful way to think about it is that your loved one has found a new best friend—a friend like no other friend, a friend who can take away distressing thoughts and emotions such as self-doubt, anxiety, and sadness. A 19-year-old female with anorexia illustrated this by saying,

For me, there was nothing else. Nothing else mattered. I didn't want my friends to call or come over. I just wanted to be with my eating disorder. I just wanted it and nothing else.

You will notice, as the eating disorder progresses, that your loved one becomes more isolated from close relationships. She no longer wants to hang out with friends. She may still be part of many types of activities, groups and organizations, but her relationships become increasingly superficial. The eating disorder eventually becomes her primary relationship—a relationship she is dependent upon and will therefore strongly defend. Your loved one resists treatment and efforts to help her because she experiences her eating disorder as a source of comfort and support. Because of this, she perceives efforts to help as a threat to this source of comfort.

What's So Hard?

You may wonder, *what does she find overwhelming enough that she would need to turn to an eating disorder to help her?* Our experience has shown us that, for the most part, emotions, her views about herself (self-concept), and relationships with others are the three main areas she feels most uncomfortable about and threatened by. Your loved one experiences these things as dangerous and threatening to her personal well-being. She sees emotions, self-concept, and relationships not as expected and natural parts of one's life but as potentially dangerous experiences—experiences that will cause her harm, and therefore experiences she believes she needs to avoid.

This may be hard to understand because for many people emotions, relationships, and how they see themselves are routine aspects of life that may not feel particularly distressing, but for someone with anorexia or bulimia, these things are extremely frightening. Because this idea can be so difficult to really understand, we will take a look in detail at emotions, self-concept, and relationships to find out what makes them seem so dangerous to your loved one. Then we will explore how the eating disorder becomes a source of comfort and support and helps her deal with her life.

Emotions

> *"I'd rather die than feel."*
>
> —Comment from a young woman with anorexia

Emotions may be painful, exciting, joyous, frightening, or any number of things. In and of themselves, they are not harmful, but people with eating disorders perceive them as frightening and even dangerous. They tend to experience emotions as a threat to their well-being and safety. A 25-year-old woman with bulimia described this poignantly.

> *When I start to feel any emotion, I just feel as though it will sweep me away like a tidal wave. It feels so powerful that I'm afraid it will hurt me, or might even kill me. I can't stand to let my feelings happen for very long before I have to do something to make them go away.*

Emotions are generally a part of everyday life as a human being. They may be pleasant, unpleasant, or something in between, but most of us expect to encounter myriad feelings during any given day. For this woman, like many others with eating disorders, emotions are experiences that threaten her very existence. Some women we spoke with acknowledged how confusing emotions are and how difficult they find knowing what to do with their emotions. They feel helpless and at the mercy of their feelings, which leads them to feel overwhelmed. These uncertainties further exacerbate their fear of emotions. The women we met with spoke very eloquently about emotions and the pain they associate with feelings. Here is some of what they said:

> *I guess I avoid emotions. I just feel that those feelings are not okay. They're not okay to share with anyone, even my parents.*

> *I have a lot of hate and anger. I have always believed it's wrong to feel hate and anger. I've always wanted them out, out of my body, and I couldn't. I just can't get past the hate.*

> *I feel a lot of loneliness and guilt. I put up a pretty good shield.... I don't like to get emotional, so I try not to feel. I just ignore them. I just pretend they don't exist. I don't like feeling that way, so I don't.*

> *It's for me the scariest things to think about. I feel that sometimes I am so full of feelings…and that emotional baggage stuff…I don't think I have room for any more, but I don't deal with them. I can't, because it's too scary and too much. I mean, I don't know what would happen if I let them out. I don't think I would stop crying.*

Emotions in general are too much for me to deal with.... When I start feeling bad or uncomfortable, I don't know what to do. I'm not very good at comforting myself.

Families and friends often wonder what eating disorders have to do with emotions. It can seem bizarre and even unbelievable that bingeing, purging, starving or over-exercising could affect what someone is feeling. In reality, eating disorders are very effective at reducing or covering up emotions. The women who spoke to us described how eating disorder behaviors make them feel calmer, more in control, and more able to deal with what is happening in their lives. In the next few chapters we describe, in detail, how bingeing, purging, starving, over-exercising, and other eating disorder behaviors act as ways of managing and dealing with emotions.

Self-Concept

> *"I have always thought I was a horrible person. I have always thought that I should be punished for things because I am a bad person."*
>
> —Comments from a young woman with anorexia

Self-concept refers to how we see ourselves in many ways, including physically, psychologically, and emotionally. People with anorexia and bulimia tend to view themselves negatively. They often feel profoundly dissatisfied and disturbed by how they see their bodies and by the kind of person they believe they are. Here are some of the things people told us:

I think I was born with a broken brain.... I never felt I was good at anything. Everyone else in my family was good at something except me.

I have a lot of insecurities, like not being good enough, not being pretty enough, not being thin enough, not working hard enough, not being real enough.

I think bad things about myself.... I have felt that it was a mistake when anything good happened to me. I didn't feel as if I deserved it.

I'm not a good enough person. I don't always have nice thoughts and I don't work hard enough. I don't deserve to have anything.

My mom is always trying to buy me things…clothes and stuff. She's always asking me what I want. Doesn't she understand that I don't deserve anything? I already feel so guilty about just being alive…. It makes me feel even guiltier when she wants to buy me something. Why doesn't she see that I'm not good enough.

You may have noticed that a common theme among people who have eating disorders is feeling not good enough. Often, someone who suffers from anorexia or bulimia considers herself an underachiever and feels that she somehow doesn't measure up in the world. This belief leaves her quite afraid because she worries that people around her will eventually discover that she is indeed inferior or damaged in some way. She fears that once they see the truth about her they will not love her or want to be around her.

Of course, it is usually obvious to her family and friends that her perception is inaccurate. Typically, however, she is so convinced that the horrible things she thinks about herself are correct that nothing can persuade her to change her beliefs. This can be very frustrating to those around her because they know that she is not inferior, that in reality she is a valuable person and that people care about her just because of who she is.

Because someone with an eating disorder tends to be so afraid of being exposed as a fraud or as someone who doesn't measure up, she will often try to cover up her negative feelings about herself. She often presents a positive image of herself to those around her to hide her negative self-concept. This strategy was common in the women we spoke with:

I try to pretend that I am confident, but I'm not.

People think that I am really strong, but I'm more on the weak side.

I mean, if you were to ask someone like my mom and dad or even my friends they would say that there's nothing wrong with me. I mean I get good grades, I have a boyfriend, I play soccer, softball…but when it comes down to it, none of it is real.... If they knew they probably wouldn't believe it.... I'm fat, ugly, I have hateful, I mean, really bad thoughts about myself. If people really knew me, really knew me, they would be shocked.

<u>Self-Concept and Body Image:</u> For people with eating disorders, body image is intimately linked with self-concept. Positive thoughts about their bodies lead to positive thoughts about themselves. Conversely, negative thoughts about their bodies contribute to feeling badly about themselves. A 20-year-old with bulimia tells us:

If I feel small in the morning when I get dressed, then I think I'm ok. If I look in the mirror and I'm fat, or my clothes don't fit, then I feel like I'm a horrible person...like I'm a failure.

The message our culture promotes that thin is good and anything other than thin is bad aggravates these feelings of low self-esteem. This perspective in society can be disturbing to many people, but those who have eating disorders are particularly affected. Here is what some girls and women said about how body image influences how they feel about themselves:

I always wanted to be stick thin.... I mean, isn't that the ideal? Isn't that what every girl tries to look like? I mean, it's the ultimate to look like a supermodel...that would mean that I was successful, that I achieved something.

Weight is really connected with how you feel about yourself. Weight goes up, you feel worse about yourself. When it comes down, you feel much better.

If I eat perfectly all day, then I feel like a good person. If I binge or eat bad things, then I feel terrible, like I'm weak and lazy and shouldn't even be here.

When I feel toned or when I am at a weight I am comfortable with, I feel good about myself.

I think if I was thin I wouldn't have to worry as much. I would feel better about myself.

I have never been happy with my body until I lose weight. I think if I was thinner I would be a lot more confident and a lot happier. I would feel a lot better about myself, and I would be more willing to do things because that's how I was when I did lose weight. When I was thin, I was really confident.

When I am thin, I feel that I am physically attractive.... Sometimes I wish I had a great body, then things would be okay and I would finally be happy. I just know that if I was thin, I would be happy.

It's like I wouldn't be a good person if I was ten pounds overweight.

I think that it was when I started high school that I somehow began feeling inadequate, not good enough. I discovered that it was not good enough to be smart or nice. I began feeling compelled to also be pretty and good looking. My appearance had mattered to me before, but somehow it became one of the most important areas in my life as it related to my level of happiness. The better I looked, the better I felt.

I see fat as being ugly and unattractive and unhappy. That's how I feel.... I am so frustrated with my body today. I feel so fat and ugly. It affects my mood and how I think of myself.

I can remember weighing ten pounds more and it was like, oh God, I'm a terrible person.

I weighed myself last night and I weigh 137 pounds. I am so fat and miserable...I feel so shitty about myself.

I'm just fat. I've tried for years to get thin enough, but I never can. It is so depressing. I'd give anything to be thin. I'm such a failure.

When I feel fat, which is most of the time, I feel horrible. I feel depressed, like I have this voice in my head telling me I'm a bad person.

I just look at my fat legs and my butt and I feel like crap...I feel like a failure, like I can't do anything right.

When I step on the scale, if I've gained weight, something clicks inside me and I feel horrible. I don't like myself.

If I got fat, I would kill myself.

The idea that body size can so influence a person's concept of herself may be difficult to comprehend. But understanding this idea can help you appreciate how capricious and unpredictable daily life is for someone who has an eating disorder. Having a self-concept based on body size is very precarious, indeed. Your loved one's perception of her body can change instantaneously, and this can immediately alter how she feels about herself as a person. A young woman with anorexia told us:

> *I can feel okay about myself, but if I walk into the house and my mom is cooking something, I instantly feel fatter. Then I feel like I'm a horrible person and I get really depressed.*

For those of us who don't have an eating disorder, how we feel about ourselves remains relatively consistent over time. Whether we have a difficult day, a really great day, or any other kind of day, we generally have the feeling that we are always the same person. This gives us a sense of stability and predictability. Most of us take this for granted and do not usually think about how reassuring it is to always know who we are. From reading the statements above, you can see that someone with an eating disorder does not experience this kind of consistency. Who she believes she is can change dramatically depending on how her clothes fit or how she sees herself in a mirror.

Relationships

> *"Relationships scare me to death. I want them, then I don't. I don't think I would know what to do if I had one. I mean, I just don't like for people to be close to me."*
>
> —Comments from a woman with anorexia

People with eating disorders often struggle enormously in relationships with friends and family. They tend to isolate themselves from others as they become more and more consumed with their eating disorders. They frequently find relating to others confusing, frightening, and distressing.

At the same time, however, girls and women who have eating disorders generally value relationships and want to have other people in their lives. They care deeply about their loved ones.

A woman with bulimia describes her experience with relationships in this way:

I don't understand it. I am so loving and I so want to be loved. But I'm always messing things up with people. I can't figure out what to do or say and I don't know what is right, it's so confusing…unpredictable really. I must not be good at it.… I feel like giving up.

Clearly, this person wants to have relationships in her life. Clearly, she also finds them confusing and difficult. When asked what she wants in a relationship she responds,

I don't know. I've never thought about it. I don't think what I want really matters—only what everybody else wants. I try to do what they want.

Other people related their experience with relationships:

I just wanted people to like me.… I couldn't get them to like me.

People thought I was really weird and I just pretended that I didn't notice, that I didn't care. But I did and it hurt.

I always felt rejected.… I didn't view myself as normal, and so I just always felt apart. I had girlfriends but nobody that was a best bud or anything. I have never had anybody that I could completely share and be intimate with.

I don't think my parents thought of me as a person.… I think I was like a piece of jewelry, like an ornament or something. I was something they were supposed to have, like a station wagon.… In our family we never touched.… I felt ignored, like I wasn't there, even though I was.

Sometimes girls and women feel that if they can't be thin enough that they will be rejected or unloved:

> *People don't like fat. I know this doesn't sound good but fat's not attractive. I mean, who's going to want to be with someone who is fat? It's just not what is considered to be attractive.*

Or:

> *I remember my mom made a comment to me about my belly after dinner one night. She then said that my boyfriend told her that he thought I would look a lot nicer if I lost ten pounds. At that moment I realized my fears had come true, others saw me as being fat.... I was afraid he was going to leave me.*

At the same time, some people believe that if they can become thin enough, their relationships will improve or they will be more loved. Consider these comments:

> *When I am thin my mom is so proud of me. She tells people I look great and I'm doing good. I know it's because I'm losing weight.*

> *When I lost weight, everyone started praising me. I was so pleased and proud. I thought I had found the key to my happiness.*

> *In the seventh grade, I got the flu and lost a lot of weight. When I went back to school, one of the popular girls asked if I lost some weight. At that moment I realized that losing weight equals being accepted.... When I lost weight, I felt more confident and I started making more friends, including boys.*

At times, relationships can be complex and demanding for anyone. In general, however, people tend to feel comforted and assured in their various kinds of relationships. In fact, many people believe that relationships are one of the most rewarding aspects of life. We can see from the comments above that relationships are seen as confusing, risky, and sometimes threatening to individuals with eating disorders. Their conflicted feelings about relationships cause them great distress. On one hand, they want to be involved with other people; on the other hand, they are quite frightened by the idea.

I Don't Know What I Would Do Without It

"It's the only thing I can trust. It helps me deal with all my shit.… It has never let me down, it has never lied to me. I mean, what else could you ask for?"

—Comments from a 22-year-old anorexic female

As the above quotes illustrate, someone with an eating disorder finds life distressing. She sees danger in many places. Life is neither fun nor safe, and her fears can become paralyzing. She is afraid of losing control of her emotions and of getting hurt in a relationship, and is afraid of and exhausted by her own thoughts. Something has to happen.

Then, something does happen—the eating disorder arrives.

The eating disorder often starts slowly. It often comes into her life looking reasonably benign. You can look at it as if the disorder approaches the person and promises to help her, without asking much in return. The disorder, in effect, offers to assist her in feeling in control, powerful, and confident. She can't refuse. At this early point, the disorder may only ask her to make minor changes in her behaviors related to food or exercise, and in return, there is a huge payoff. The distressing thoughts and feelings are taken away. They may not be completely gone, but enough for the person to experience some relief. To maintain this, all she has to do is comply with the eating disorder's requests.

Family members or friends may not even notice any changes this early on in the disorder, or it may just look like their loved one is trying to eat in a healthy way or to lose a little weight. In fact, the person herself at this point may not even feel very different; she may believe that she's only making minor adjustments to her lifestyle.

However, soon the eating disorder begins to demand more from her. As the weeks progress, she feels like she needs to make more dramatic changes to her food and/or exercise behaviors. What is happening is that the eating disorder, in effect, is telling her that she must do more for it if she wants it to continue to help her feel okay. Unfortunately, the disorder constantly demands more from the person in return for continuing to help her with her distressing thoughts and emotions.

The eating disorder becomes more entrenched in the person's life, and it takes a greater toll on her. As the severity of the eating disorder increases, the person becomes more reluctant to let go of it for fear of returning to the way things were before.

It may seem strange to think of the eating disorder as a friend. What kind of friend would treat your loved one so badly? But people with eating disorders often experience the disorder as a friend. They tend to focus on how much the disorder helps them and how consistent and reliable they find the disorder. We have often heard people say that the disorder will never let them down and will never surprise them. They know how the disorder behaves and what it asks of them, and they know what it will give them if they simply do what it says.

4

I'm Anorexic

People with anorexia restrict their food intake, count calories, excessively exercise, and sometimes purge because they believe by doing so they will feel better about themselves, not experience distressing emotions, and have better relationships.

Girls and women who have anorexia hope that if they look and feel thin enough, their lives will be dramatically different and better. Because of these beliefs and hopes, doing whatever it takes to lose weight and achieve a sense of thinness becomes the fundamental goal of someone with this disorder.

Unfortunately, this strategy is problematic. Most often, someone with anorexia never reaches a weight or body size that she believes is thin enough. Even if she feels satisfied for a brief time that she has achieved an acceptable level of thinness, her satisfaction is generally quite short lived. Soon feelings of distress about herself and her life return, and so does her conviction that if she can just reach that magic number or size, the distress will disappear. These are some things people who spoke to us had to say about this vicious cycle:

> *Over the years my goal, what I wanted to weigh, has gotten lower. I keep thinking it will get better.... Someday I will feel good about my body and I will be, you know, happy. Maybe not hysterically happy, but I will feel good about my life. I don't ever feel good, like I think you're supposed to feel.... When I do lose some weight, any weight, I feel better. Not great, but better.*

I have a weight—a weight that I want to get to. I know I'll feel better when I get there.

Once I started losing the weight, then the more weight I lost, the more terrified I was of gaining anything back because I felt like everything I was getting out of it would be taken away.

I lost weight, I know that, but I still have a ways to go.... It hasn't led to me feeling better.

My goal weight gets lower and lower.

I don't know what it's about, but I have a weight I want to be at and I know things will be better, I will feel better about myself.

Doesn't She See What She is Doing?

For family and friends, the fact that someone can lose weight and become sickly thin and not realize it is one of the more confusing and frustrating aspects of anorexia. It seems inconceivable that a person would not recognize a severe change of body size. We have often heard loved ones ask, "She must see that she is too small, how could she not?" and "Why won't she admit how thin she really is?"

But, the person with anorexia is not lying or being contrary or rebellious about what she sees in the mirror; she looks at herself and sees someone who is simply not thin enough.

What Is She Trying To Accomplish?

So, if girls and women who have anorexia cannot see themselves accurately when it comes to their weight and body size, and if actual numbers do not convince them of what is really going on with their bodies, how do they measure their "thinness"? This is a very important question, and understanding the way someone with anorexia is assessing herself may be of great help to you as a friend or family member.

For her, thinness is measured primarily by how she feels. She believes she is thin when she *feels* thin. What a scale might say, what you or anyone else might tell her, is, for the most part, irrelevant. Most of the time she simply will not believe anything other than what she subjectively experiences. One young woman insisted, despite anything her doctors, friends or relatives told her, that she was "just *huge*" and "disgusting," even though in reality she was significantly underweight. When someone would ask her how she could possibly believe she was overweight, she replied that she "knew" she was fat because "I feel it."

Regardless of their body weight, people with anorexia rarely feel thin. Some people see their entire bodies as too large, whereas others may be dissatisfied with specific parts of their bodies. An emaciated woman stated, "I have fat everywhere, especially on my back and stomach." Others said,

> *I have never looked in the mirror and seen what anyone else sees. I have never seen a thin person.*

> *I would feel my bones and stuff, and I liked that I could feel certain bones sticking out and like when I took a bath it hurt because I was so thin. I always think parts of me are fat. I thought my legs were fat, my thighs and my hips. I thought my arms were thin, but parts of me I just thought were never going to get thin.... I always feel like I could lose more weight. I wouldn't mind being thinner. I always think that my hips are too big.*

> *I look down at me right now and I am huge. I hesitate to take off my shirt because I know that I am wearing a tank top and have the flabbiest arms.*

It can be extremely frustrating to have a conversation with someone who cannot see what is really happening to her. But what the statements above so vividly illustrate is the frustration, agony, and insecurity the person who has anorexia lives with each and every moment.

How Does She Think Feeling Thin Will Help?

We have said that someone with anorexia attempts to deal with experiences she finds difficult or frightening by trying to attain a particular weight and by doing whatever she can to experience her body as thin. But how does feeling thin help her deal with these difficult situations?

It Helps Me Not Feel

For one thing, the primary method she uses to achieve "thinness" is by limiting the amount of food she eats. Severely restricting food intake has dramatic implications for any of us. Too little nutrition negatively affects concentration, memory, and thought processes, but it also makes someone feel "numb" or "out of touch" or "in a different zone." It turns out that this "numbness" is extremely important to the person who has anorexia. The numbness that results from restricting her food considerably decreases her awareness of distressing emotions. Because the emotions that are too painful or difficult are lessened or eliminated, she feels safer and less vulnerable. She feels calm and as if she has everything under control. For the most part, as long as she continues to restrict her food intake, she can maintain this numb state.

The women we spoke with were quite articulate about how the anorexia affected them and how it made them feel. Many had a sophisticated awareness of how their disorder muted or diminished their emotions.

> *When I don't eat I just feel flat-lined. It's like I'm made of rubber or something—I just have no emotions.*

> *It's kind of addictive—feeling in that zone I get into when I don't eat, or don't eat enough.... I miss that place when I am not there.*

> *It has always been easier for me to deal with physical pain, so if I feel some pain because I'm not eating, that's okay with me. That is probably why I cut on myself, because I'd rather deal with the physical pain than the emotional pain.*

> *When I am really into it, I don't feel a lot.... I don't feel—physically or emotionally.*

I Feel Better About Myself

In addition, restricting her food reduces her life to just a few thoughts, such as: "How can I avoid eating?" "How much weight can I lose?" "What should my perfect weight be?" and "How far can I run today?" By focusing only on weight and food-related matters, she avoids thinking about and therefore facing the many complexities, uncertainties, and demanding decisions that make up life. This gives her the impression she very much desires: that her life is stable and secure.

Furthermore, her ability to restrict food often leads to feelings she finds positive. Some examples include feeling in control, feeling like she is a powerful and strong person, and having the sense that things in her life are predictable and safe. It alters her perception of the world, as well as her self-concept. Here are some examples of what we heard:

> *For some reason, being thin, being the thinnest, is something that I have control of.*

> *Being thin, as thin as I am, gives me a sense of power or control over my body.*

> *I feel like I'm happier. I just feel stronger and better. I feel proud, like I can do that. I can control that. I feel strong.*

> *It kind of made me feel like I was kind of powerful in a way. Like I could go all this time without eating.*

> *It was clearly a way for me to feel some control in my life. It was something that my parents couldn't control.*

> *Not giving in to the hunger gives me a sense of power.*

> *I felt like I could do something no one else could. I would see people eating and think to myself, I didn't have to do that and they did.*

Some people view being thin as a way of attaining or increasing a sense of self-worth, as a way to feel special or unique, or as a way of securing a sense of happiness. It becomes a way for them to alter their negative self-concepts. Some illustrations of this perspective are:

> *I figured if I couldn't be the prettiest, then I would be the thinnest. Something to make me unique or special.*

> *It's real clear for me, I want to be thin because that's what other people want, and it matters to me what other people think of me.*

> *I want to be thin because I want to be attractive. You know, it's the attractive women that have the happy endings. The ugly women never have the happy endings. In the fairy tales, the ugly women are the ones that get cooked in the oven and stuff like that.*

> *I never felt good about myself or like there was anything special about me. When I first lost weight, people noticed, and so then I thought that was something that people would notice about me. I would get attention for it, not only from my family but from everyone. It was a way for me to be special.*

It Helps Me With My Relationships

Finally, the person with anorexia believes that experiencing herself as thin will help her deal with the anxiety she feels around relationships. It either gives her more confidence to engage in relationships or more often gives her a sense that she does not need relationships. For many anorexics, relationships become a hassle and are thus avoided. As examples of this, consider the following:

> *I have always thought that if I was thin I would fit in more.... Being thin is what guys want. If men didn't want thin women, it wouldn't be in all the magazines or on TV.*

> *Being thin or having a nice body will get you a lot. People like thin. I knew that I had the boyfriends I had in part because what I looked like...the fact that I was thin.*

> *People like thin people. Guys like thin girls. Girls envy other girls who are thin. As long as I am thin, I will have something.*

If I was fat, I couldn't have people see me. I couldn't have relationships. I couldn't have people touch me.

This boyfriend I had, he liked thin women. I always felt that I had to be thin for him. When our relationship started going bad, he started to see other women…and that was really hard for me. I figured that if I couldn't be prettier than the women he was seeing, I could be thinner, so I stopped eating.

As a way of avoiding relationships, consider these comments:

I used to like being around people. I mean, in high school I was always out doing stuff with my friends. Now they don't call anymore because I've been avoiding them…. I think that's just as well…. The eating disorder takes a lot of my time.

I really don't need anyone right now in my life.

I think they [relationships] cause me more grief than it's worth.

Isn't It Just Food?

For many people, food is a relatively simple thing. For example, an apple is pretty much just an apple. It may be a food we like, dislike, or don't care about one way or another, but it does not generally hold a moral value for us or frighten us. But for someone who has anorexia, an apple has meaning far beyond being just a piece of fruit.

The complex and powerful meanings food has for people with anorexia influence how she thinks about and behaves around food. She may see some foods as "good" or "safe" and others as "bad" or "evil," and she often assumes that food is actually going to try to harm her by causing her to gain weight. Unfortunately, her relationship with food can become increasingly agonizing as the disorder progresses. Some of the women shared their experiences this way:

I wish I could just take food at face value…. I'm so afraid of it. Even something like a grape seems so dangerous to me…. Like it will damage me in some way if I eat it.

I just don't get it—how can someone even think of eating a piece of pizza? I can't even imagine putting that grease and fat into my mouth. I'd never do that in a million years. I'd rather die.

I used to do really strange things with food. At first I couldn't be around food at all. I didn't like go to the grocery store for like almost 2 months. I had no food in the house, nothing. I used to see people eating and it would just make me sick.

I love food. I love it and I hate it…. It drives me crazy because it's always on my mind. I love to feed people and I love to cook, but for me food is bad because it will make me fat.

When I eat, nobody is around and it is dark. I don't want to look at my food. I don't like to think about eating it. I don't even eat with my boy-friend. I can't even eat with my boyfriend because I don't like to hear him eat. I am very critical of what he eats, and I get mad at him because I can't eat.

When I first started with my eating disorder most things were still okay…. Then certain meats became bad, then all meat, then milk stuff…then even fruits became off limits. And after awhile, I was afraid to put anything into my mouth. Once something becomes a bad food, then it is always off limits. I can't make it okay again.

When I was a kid, I could eat anything I wanted and not even think about it. Foods weren't good or bad. I don't know what changed—I don't get it. I know intellectually that a food shouldn't be bad or good, but I don't feel that way at all.

My mom makes this casserole that has cheese on top of it. She doesn't understand why I can't have any. I don't understand how she can think that cheese is safe to eat; it is such a bad food.

Food is a source of enormous distress for many people with anorexia. Consider the following:

If I don't eat, then I feel really powerful—like nothing can harm me. But if I eat anything, even a piece of fruit, then everything comes crashing down around me and is ruined. I feel weak and like I can't do anything.

When I do eat, I feel like a failure. It's the worst feeling in the world to have food in my stomach.

If I don't eat, then it is a good day and I feel really strong. But if I give in and eat, then the whole day is ruined, and I feel like a loser.

Eating food, gaining weight, makes me very anxious. To stop the anxiety and the fear, I don't eat.

At the time, eating is pleasurable. Then when I am done and it is all over with, then I start to feel fear and anger.

I can't eat like normal people eat.... I don't even like to think about it...it's too scary.

When I am not eating, I feel that I am in control. When I do eat, I feel that I lose that control and I want to get it back.

Friends and family can have difficulty in appreciating how a food can hold more meaning than just being a food. We have seen families become frustrated and even feel like giving up because they can't understand why their loved one is afraid of something like a tablespoon of butter. Even if you cannot truly understand how butter could be frightening, remembering that your loved one experiences it as scary and threatening will go a long way toward facilitating communication between the two of you. In addition, she will be grateful that you are attempting to see things as she does, no matter how difficult that may be.

Do I Have To Watch Out For Other Eating Disorder Behaviors?

Bingeing and purging is generally thought of as a part of bulimia. Purging, however, is not uncommon in anorexia. There is a difference between purging seen in anorexia and that found in bulimia for some girls and women. Those who have bulimia more often than not consume relatively large amounts of food when they binge, whereas those with anorexia tend to feel that even small amounts of food necessitate purging. Several women told us,

> *If I think I've eaten more than 500 calories in a day, I will purge everything else I might eat. It seems that anytime I put anything in my mouth I think that I ate too much. My limit seems to be two bites.*

> *If I eat anything other than my veggies, I usually will throw it up.*

> *It's like, for me, it could be anything. I mean, it's more like a feeling. A feeling that I ate too much. I don't have to eat a lot. I mean, I could be having my cabbage soup and think I should purge.*

> *It depends on how I'm feeling that day—what kind of day I'm having. Sometimes I can eat some things, then other times I have to throw up when all I have is a glass of water.*

> *It could be anything, a bagel or a muffin. It's not what you think a binge should be.*

Hear Their Stories

To put this all in context, we will tell the stories of two women. Katy and Jaquie are as unique as any of the rest of us; therefore, their stories are unique. At the same time, however, their experiences with anorexia are similar in many ways to what others with this disorder face.

I'm Katy

Katy came to treatment at age 15, when she was a sophomore in high school. Her parents were worried that Katy's health was suffering and that her behavior was beyond her control. Katy was angry that her parents were making her begin treatment. She did not think there was anything wrong with her, and she felt she had too much to do to be spending time "talking to strangers about nothing."

But, despite Katy's insistence that nothing was wrong with her, it was apparent that she was in the throes of an eating disorder. When Katy was 13, she began to limit what she would let herself eat. At first she gave up meat, feeling like she just wanted to "eat healthier" and get into better shape. Then she began to limit foods with fat, such as dairy and desserts. Her parents became worried when Katy's weight began to drop. Katy tried to reassure them that nothing was wrong.

Katy's parents had divorced when she was young, and she was not close to either one of them at this point. She resented them for breaking up the family, which also included her two brothers—one older and one slightly younger. Katy lived mostly with her mother but stayed with her father some weekends and holidays.

Katy was an athlete in junior high school. She ran track and played basketball. Feeling like she needed more exercise than she got in school sports, she added extra running in the evenings and on weekends.

Becoming increasingly concerned about their daughter, Katy's parents took her to the family physician. All her blood work was normal, and Katy's weight, although it had dropped several pounds, was not particularly low.

When Katy began high school, things only got worse. High school meant new friends, new situations, and more schoolwork. Katy had always been a very good student, but she began to feel inadequate and worried that she wouldn't be able to keep up with her classmates nor get into college. She felt anxious and nervous about school and about her friends. She worried that people didn't really like her, and she felt lonely and left out at school. She also felt that her body was out of control, that it was fat and ugly. She desperately wanted to lose weight and thought that if she could just get thinner, everyone would like her more and that life would be easier.

Her fears that she wasn't liked and that she might not be smart enough for college humiliated Katy. No one could understand why she thought these things about herself. Her friends and family always told her that she was well liked and very intelligent, but Katy thought something must be inherently wrong with her—that she had some flaw in her character that people simply had not discovered. She was certain that someone would inevitably discover the flaw and would then understand "what a loser" she was. Katy did not want anyone to know how awful she felt about herself and that she was hiding this "flaw," so she tried to look as if everything was going well. She pretended she was happy and that nothing bothered her.

What Katy felt the best about was her ability to control what she ate. No matter what else happened during the day, she could count on being able to choose what and how much she would eat. She could also control her exercise. Katy found herself spending more time exercising and less time with friends. It was easy to say "no" to doing things with her friends because she felt that they didn't really want to be around her anyway. She didn't feel like being social—too much work and too tiring. She would sit with her friends at lunch, but she generally turned down all weekend or after-school activities, particularly anything where food might be involved.

Katy's days became intensely involved with food. It wasn't the eating of it, though, that was taking up her time. Katy recalled, "It was the constant thinking about food, the planning of what I would let myself eat, the comparing myself to others and what they ate and what I thought they probably weighed." It was very time consuming and exhausting. But there was something about it that Katy actually liked: "It gave me something to focus on, something I could have control over. I loved that. I hated unpredictability." She couldn't help it if people might not like her, or if she couldn't get along with her parents, or if they had gotten a divorce, but she could certainly control her body, and that was a huge relief. If she could just get thin enough, everything would be okay.

Katy continued to restrict her food intake, so by the end of her freshman year she only ate fruit and some non-fat yogurt during the day. Much of her energy came from diet soft drinks that contained caffeine. She had lost a significant amount of weight by this time, but Katy did not feel thin. She told us, "I still felt I was overweight and disgusting, and that I just needed to work harder to get thinner. I was convinced that if I just worked hard enough, I could get there."

Katy's parents tried to get her to eat. They bought her favorite foods, took her out to restaurants she had liked in the past, and sometimes even threatened to take away certain privileges if she didn't resume eating, but the more her parents pressed, the more resolute Katy became about not eating. She was angry with her parents for trying to make her eat. Later she recalled, "They didn't understand how important this was to me, and I wasn't going to give in to them. They might be able to make me do some things, but they couldn't make me eat." Her friends were also worried, but Katy felt they just pitied her or that they were jealous that she could go without eating.

By this time, Katy's metabolism had slowed down considerably as her body tried to adjust to being given such a small amount of food. Katy was running largely on the adrenaline her body was releasing to help it cope with not having enough nutrition and on caffeine. She actually felt pretty good—better than she had before she began limiting what she ate. Back then she felt anxious, uncomfortable, and fearful. Now she just felt kind of numb, like not much mattered.

> I loved my eating disorder. I mean, I didn't have to
> deal. The worries, the anxiety or whatever just
> wasn't there anymore.... It felt good to be numb.

Katy drifted through her days, not paying much attention to what was going on around her and not really caring, either. She actually felt pretty energetic, thanks to the adrenaline and lots of caffeine. This seemed like a much better situation to her. "It was a relief. Everything had felt so complicated to me for so long. And hard. And scary, I think. But now, my main focus was how much I weighed and getting that number to go lower and lower."

By this time, Katy's parents were quite concerned. They insisted that Katy begin treatment, and Katy was diagnosed with anorexia nervosa.

Here Is How It Worked For Katy

Katy's anorexia began slowly and was seemingly innocent. She just wanted to "get into better shape" and "eat healthier." However, rather quickly, her relationship with food and eating turned into something much more powerful and dangerous. Avoiding food became Katy's primary way of dealing with her life.

By not eating and exercising excessively, the anxiety, fear, and distress that she felt, particularly once she started high school, decreased. Furthermore, her eating and exercise behaviors became increasingly effective in covering up what she really felt. Limiting her food intake and exercising excessively made her feel better about her body, which in turn increased her self-esteem and confidence. In essence, her eating disorder came into her life and took all the "bad" away.

Anorexia moved in, unbeknownst to Katy. It all happened very quietly—so quietly that Katy didn't even notice at first. Katy did not wake up one day and say, "Oh, I think I'll use anorexia as a way to make myself feel safer and make life seem more predictable." Eating disorders don't begin that way. Somewhere inside, Katy knew she was in trouble and that something had to happen to help her feel more stable. She used not eating as a way of managing emotions she found threatening to her, thus her eating disorder became a resource, a support, and even an ally. She did not see it as destructive, but as a friend helping her through tough times.

In response to Katy's behavior, her parents tried to make her eat. Their reaction was, of course, normal for any loving parent or other loved one. However, Katy viewed her parents' attempts to get her to eat as threatening. She experienced their insistence that she eat as "trying to make me fat" again. But really, if Katy began to eat, she would begin to feel again, and she did not want to feel. She didn't want to be faced with all those overwhelming emotions; after all, with the help of her eating disorder, she had gotten rid of them, and things seemed so much better without them. It was vital that she resist eating.

Her parents, understandably, were confused, frustrated, and worried. They could not comprehend why their daughter wouldn't eat. Eating seemed so natural to them, so necessary and so benign. But to Katy, eating felt dangerous and potentially fatal.

Katy's resistance to treatment was also understandable. She saw treatment as a threat, partly because it might entail eating, but also because she was afraid of what "getting better" might mean. She had become so accustomed to this way of being, and she felt secure. She couldn't imagine how else to live.

> *I was terrified to begin eating. I would have done anything to get out of it. I would have rather died than eat.... I could not imagine my life without my eating disorder.*

Anorexia had become her friend, and it helped her cope with her thoughts and feelings. It provided her with relief and an escape from her distress. She was extremely afraid that without it she would be left defenseless and would not be able to survive. Because she was prone to feeling inadequate, she doubted her ability to find and develop any other way to cope.

> *Now that I look back on it, I was really afraid I was going to die. I thought I was only afraid I was going to be fat, but now I realize that I felt if I didn't have my anorexia that I wouldn't exist. I felt I was nothing without it. It became everything to me.*

I'm Jaquie

Jaquie is an 18-year-old recent graduate from high school. She plans to attend college and pursue a degree in history. Her long-term goal is to become a high school teacher.

Jaquie's parents divorced when she was 7 years old. Her father moved into a nearby apartment and initially remained a big part of Jaquie's life. As time went on, however, she saw her father less and less. He got a job that required him to travel, and he was often out of town for up to two weeks at a time. She admits that her parents' divorce impacted her greatly. She missed seeing her father and missed seeing her parents together. Her father eventually remarried and moved to another town. Jaquie visited him and his new family once a month and remembers feeling like she was an "outsider" or a "guest," and not a member of the family. Her mother did not remarry nor did she date after the divorce.

Jaquie had begun dancing when she was 10 years old and immediately fell in love with it. It wasn't long before she was taking three to four classes a week. She recalls that dance gave her a way to "escape life." While she was dancing, nothing else mattered.

Increasingly, Jaquie's life revolved around dance. Her mother remembers that Jaquie frequently talked about becoming a professional dancer and touring all over the world. Her mother also acknowledged that dance gave her a way of staying close to her daughter. She took Jaquie to her dance classes and to performances, giving mother and daughter plenty of time together.

Jaquie was developing into a fine dancer. She had won several awards at competitions, and her teachers frequently commented on her natural abilities. But all was not perfect. One day a teacher commented to Jaquie that she thought Jaquie had gained some weight. In addition, she said she hoped Jaquie did not develop large breasts because that would interfere with her ability to continue dancing at a competitive level. At this same time, she overheard her aunt tell her mother that she thought Jaquie had gained some weight and that she'd better watch out because "boys don't like heavy girls." In response to these comments, Jaquie remembers feeling an intense fear that she had become fat, that she wouldn't be able to dance anymore, and that she would never have a boyfriend.

She decided at that point that she would stop eating. She was determined not to be fat and not to let anything interfere with her ability to dance. Jaquie began to severely restrict her food intake. She ate less than 1000 calories per day and continued to dance almost daily. At first, she felt ravenous and thought about food all the time. Nevertheless, she stayed below her calorie limit and only ate foods low in fat. She would deal with food cravings by buying the food she desired, chewing it so she would get the taste, and then spitting it out so she wouldn't have to count the calories. As time went on and her eating disorder developed further, she had fewer food cravings, and she found it increasingly easy to eat very little.

As expected, Jaquie began losing weight, and her dance instructors commented that she looked better and seemed to be dancing better. In addition, she received admiration from other dancers on her ability to be so disciplined regarding what she ate. Jaquie recalls that at this time she was fully consumed by her eating disorder.

It wasn't long before Jaquie's mother became concerned about her daughter's weight loss and "obsession" with food and weight. When she approached her about her concerns, Jaquie responded with intense anger. Her mother spoke to others about her concerns and typically received the response that Jaquie had a dancer's body and not to worry. It wasn't until Jaquie collapsed one day in practice that people took notice of her physical condition.

Jaquie was asked to leave the team because the dance company felt that if she continued to dance she would be risking her health. At this point, the eating disorder was controlling her. She couldn't stop, even if continuing her anorexia meant not being able to dance any longer.

She did leave the team, but her eating disorder didn't leave her. Instead, she remained consumed with fears of gaining weight. Her fears were exacerbated when she realized that without dancing she had no way of burning calories. She began to exercise. Her regimen included running three to four miles every other day and riding her bike on alternate days. In addition, she would do aerobics at home on days she "felt fat."

Here Is How It Worked For Jaquie

Jaquie's identity was based upon her ability to dance. Her ability to dance gave her a sense of belonging and of purpose in her life, and it was something she felt passionate about. In addition, she danced to relieve her day-to-day pressures and struggles and to drown out her feelings about her parents' divorce and the diminishing role her father played in her life. In essence, dancing was the way she coped.

Jaquie felt the dance instructor's comments about her weight and body threatened her dancing. Therefore, she also considered them threats to her ability to cope with life's stresses. Jaquie interpreted the teacher's comments as an almost direct demand for her to do something about her body. If she was getting "too fat to dance," then it was up to her to prevent that from happening.

It made sense to Jaquie to eat less and exercise more to make sure her body stayed within her control. Unfortunately, as she began to lose weight, she began coping with life through her quest to be thin. Her eating disorder helped her deal with distressing thoughts and feelings.

Throughout her life, Jaquie had struggled with her self-confidence, and often felt that she lacked things that others had. She never felt as if she was as smart or as pretty as others. She dealt with these feelings through dancing. When she danced, she felt good about herself. Jaquie felt that she did measure up to others and, at times, even felt that she was much better than her peers.

The effect dance had on Jaquie was lost when she realized that it could be taken away. If she became "fat" or developed physically, she could lose her ability to dance at the level she desired. She began to feel that she didn't have control over her dance and the ability to use it as a way of feeling good about herself.

The one thing Jaquie ultimately did control was her eating, so her way of coping changed from dancing to something she felt she had more control over: whether or not she ate.

If she experienced herself as "thin enough," she believed she would feel better about herself and be more secure in her life. Unfortunately, Jaquie seldom felt thin, regardless of how much she weighed. If she ever did feel thin, it was short lived. By this point, Jaquie did not know any other way to cope with her life. Her anorexia had become firmly embedded in her identity, and had become her way of coping. Because of this, she continued to cling to the disorder. For Jaquie, her anorexia was never a problem. Instead, it was a solution to a problem.

Conclusion

As Katy, Jaquie, and the other girls and women in this chapter illustrate to us, to feel safe and in control of their lives they relied on their belief that everything would be okay if they could only become thin enough. You can see that restricting their food intake, exercising excessively to burn calories, and, for some, purging, are their ways of trying to avoid what they experience as threatening to them. The eating disorder behaviors become a way to cope—a friend who will help them through difficult times. A friend they are reluctant to give up because without it they fear they will be overwhelmed with negative thoughts and emotions, and the demands of relationships.

5

I'm Bulimic

Whereas people with anorexia restrict their food intake as a coping strategy, those with bulimia use bingeing and purging as the primary method
of dealing with situations and conditions they feel are threatening. In individuals with anorexia, as well as those with bulimia, their emotions, relationships, and self-concept become threats to their personal well-being.

Individuals who have anorexia think that if they can just not eat, everything will be okay. People with bulimia, however, have a more complicated and contradictory relationship with food. They see food both as a
salvation and as a danger. These conflicted feelings about food and eating
account for the cycle of bingeing and then purging.

The women we spoke with told us that eating seemed to provide comfort
and a sense of security. They felt it "numbed them out" and calmed them
down. These beliefs about what food could do led them to binge. However, after bingeing, panic overtook them and drove them to purge the
food that by now felt dangerous and harmful. But as we will see, although
panic over having just "eaten a ton" may spark purging, this behavior also
may help someone feel comforted and soothed. It becomes a source of
comfort, as one friend comforts another. A 20-year-old told us,

> *I'll be so anxious that all I can think of is eating and eating. For a few*
> *minutes it helps, and I feel better. But then it all starts to crash in on me*
> *again…all the anxiety and dread. But it's worse then because I also feel*
> *guilty about having eaten all that. So I'm really screwed at this point. But*
> *then I start to purge, and that makes me feel calmer again for awhile. I*
> *really don't know what I would do without it.*

This cycle of needing to eat but then panicking and having to purge is confusing and frightening. Many people we spoke with told us they felt "crazy" or "messed up inside." They couldn't figure out what was happening to them or how to make it stop.

What Causes Her To Binge?

Though a variety of circumstances can lead someone to binge, a common thread is that the person feels distressed and threatened: Perhaps a problem in a relationship; a bad day at work; feelings of anxiety, frustration, or anger; negative thoughts or feelings about who she is as a person; or even physical discomfort or pain will bring on distress. When one of these difficult experiences arises, she turns to bingeing as a way to cope.

Usually, I am really confused about something, and I am trying to thrash it out in my mind. During these times, I am more likely to binge. When my spirits are up, I am not as focused on food.

Before bingeing, I was really upset. I mean, I was really down on myself.

Before I binge, I usually start having all these thoughts running through my head. I start thinking of all the stuff I have to do and how behind I am.

I had a real shitty day at work. I mean, I did this real bonehead thing. I told something to this guy that I wasn't supposed to. It wasn't that big of a deal, but when I got home I was really down on myself for it.

This fear, this anxiety—the kind that causes me to stutter and forget words—developed with my eating disorder. I don't know how it ties in. I do know the less anxiety I experience, the less bingeing I do.

If my heart hurts, I will go binge.

When I am at my parents' house, I binge and purge twice as much as I normally do. When I am there, I feel a tremendous amount of pressure. I feel that everything around me is oppressing me. I don't go to my dad's house much because when I am there I eat and throw up. I feel very uncomfortable there. I can't be myself. I don't feel that I am accepted by him.

Before this last binge, I was feeling real depressed and out of control about a conversation I had with my mother.... There are certain reasons why I binge and it's like when I am tired, when I am angry, and when I am lonely. These are the emotions I have to watch out for.

I was really upset. My mind started racing, and I was thinking of all kinds of things. I felt like I was losing control because I could not do everything I needed to get done. I am having all of these emotions and feelings, and I feel like I am trapped. I know if I don't get all these things done, I will feel like a failure.

There's lots going on. I mean, there's a part of me that's trying to talk myself out of bingeing.... I don't want to do it, but it's like I have to. I have all these thoughts running through my head. It's like they're going a million miles an hour. I'm also usually feeling really anxious, maybe even scared.... I don't know why I'm feeling that, but I just know that I do.

It Makes Me Feel Better

Food and eating hold symbolic and unique meanings for people with bulimia. Many of the women we spoke to acknowledged that they often eat when they are not physically hungry. They eat to fulfill other needs, a state many described as "emotionally hungry." Some of what they were "hungry" for was comfort, security, or relief from pain, anger, confusion, or other difficult emotions. Here are some things they told us:

I use food for comfort. I don't use food for energy.... I look at people who eat well or who eat because they are hungry and I am so envious.

Food is really comforting to me, it is fulfilling.

For me, food means security. Like if I knew there was food there whenever I wanted it, I feel security around that. I guess it is comforting...in a way, it's real controllable.

I have always viewed certain foods as a sign of success. You're making the money, you can eat well.

I Don't Binge On Just Anything

Just like the act of bingeing itself, the foods someone chooses to eat during a binge may have special meaning to her that contribute to her eating disorder. Some people choose almost exclusively foods high in fat or sugar, whereas for others, traditional meals such as steak and potatoes or macaroni and cheese are typical binge foods. Someone who is trying to comfort herself by bingeing might gravitate toward foods that were a source of comfort when she was younger. For someone else, foods that were not allowed when she was a child might be her first choice.

No matter what specific meaning binge foods hold, in general, they tend to be foods someone usually denies herself. Typically, she will not allow herself these foods on a regular basis because they are high in fat and calories, and perceived to cause weight gain.

I enjoy food. I don't allow myself to have treats. For example, I love sweets, so I feel that if I would say, "Okay, every Friday or every once in a while enjoy it, treat yourself." See, then I would want more, I want more. I want it whenever I want it, but I don't want to suffer the consequences.

I will just be eating and then I will say, "You know, you really want that cookie." I knew in my reasoning that once I had that fattening cookie I was going to binge, but my hand was already reaching for that cookie. I know I shouldn't, but I rationalize it, like I say, "Oh, you can exercise and work it off."

I was in the mood for sweets.... It's like sometimes I've got to have my sweets. I don't do it too often, because if I didn't get rid of it through purging I would get fat.... So I went to the store and bought a half gallon of chocolate chip ice cream and two candy bars. I went home and had two big bowls of ice cream and the candy.

I was eating maybe 400 calories a day. I was obsessed with food while I was obsessed with being thin or losing weight.... I would create elaborate, fattening meals or desserts and eat just one or two bites and give the rest to my family.... On Halloween night I got drunk...and ate two or three bags of candy.... I have always been a really big eater. I love fattening foods.... I started these weird habits where I would eat food and spit it out. I used to buy donuts or candy and eat it and spit it out on the ground.

The amount of food someone eats in a binge varies greatly. Some people consume what might be considered an extraordinary amount of food. Others think of a binge as what many people consider a typical meal, and some feel that anything they eat constitutes a binge. And what makes this all the more complicated is that the criteria for whether something is a binge can change over time, even day by day or within a particular day.

Often "crossing the line" determines whether something is a binge or not. The "line" is the point where she feels she has eaten too much and that she is going to have to make herself purge. The "line" is a point that is different for each person. Furthermore, where the line is can vary at times for the same person.

For one person, the line might be when she feels full. For another, it might be when she realizes she has eaten a certain number of calories or a particular food that she considers "bad." One person told us,

Any time I can feel my pants touching me I know I have had too much. Especially if they touch my stomach. Once I notice that, then I just eat anything, because I know I am going to purge.

Someone can't always tell if she is getting near the line; it can sneak up on her suddenly. But once she has crossed that line, stopping herself from eating more or stopping herself from purging is extremely difficult.

Anything for me can be a binge.... It's just when I think I've eaten too much.... That could be a muffin or bagel or a full meal.

I figure if I'm going to binge, I might as well. I mean, I think about foods I haven't eaten because they are bad foods and I go get them because I know I'm just going to get rid of it.... When I do that, I stuff myself. I feel uncomfortably full.

I can go to a dinner party and I will have something that is really minimal. It certainly isn't enough that I feel bad about it, but if I eat a little bit too much, then I will indulge in everything, and I will eat like there is no tomorrow.

After the first plate of spaghetti, I was thinking that I could feel a little guilty about having two dinners. I could just let it go or I could give in to my desires and eat anything I wanted. I figured that I crossed the line, so I might as well keep going.

It's like I am eating and I take the next bite and I have gone over the edge...and I can't stop.

It's A Way I Can Get Away From It All

When someone binges, whatever is going on around her seems to stand still. The person now becomes preoccupied with eating and doesn't have to focus on whatever she was thinking about or feeling before she started eating. In addition, the act of bingeing makes her feel "numb," "anesthetized," or "in another zone" where she is not very aware of anything she might be feeling. Someone with bulimia considers this state much more tolerable than what she was experiencing before the binge. Whatever feelings she had before she began eating felt threatening. She begins eating and suddenly things change. Some examples:

I watch TV when I binge. I watch movies. I close the door, lock it, put down the blinds, turn on the TV, and it is just like a total escape. It's like my mind is free. I am totally in a world of my own. It is like I am happy, comfortable. I am content.

I sometimes almost get excited about bingeing because I know I am going to get an adrenaline rush. The feeling that I get during a binge is like taking a drug. It is very soothing, very nurturing, and it feels good.

I am hungry, and just not physically but emotionally, in a way, I think. By the end of the day, I have just felt so much shit I just feel worn down, and I eat to mellow out a little bit.... It feels good. The bingeing feels good, eating feels good, it makes me feel good.

It is like I am not conscious during the binge. It's not until after I have eaten I realize that I shouldn't have done that.

Bingeing numbs me of emotions and thoughts.

When I am bingeing, I am not recognizing what I am feeling.

I become a total space case when I am eating. I can eat a huge bowl of popcorn and be gone, totally out of my body, almost like an out-of-body experience.

I never remember a binge afterwards.... It's like I am checked out during binges.

I always feel possessed when I am bingeing. I feel like I am observing myself.

It's a numb feeling. The only thing I can compare it to is like having a buzz. I am not connected to anything in reality. I am just like kind of numb and sitting back and observing everything. Like even observing myself.

If It Would Only Last

But the reprieve is short lived. After the binge, the same old feelings and thoughts return, and so does her need to do something about them. The binge allowed her to only momentarily escape those feelings.

Some people told us that their emotions actually intensified after bingeing. In addition to trying to cope with those feelings that had already been there, they now also had to deal with the guilt of having just binged and the worry that they would gain weight.

My mood gets worse after I binge. I feel really disgusted with myself for bingeing.... I know what I did will make me fat, and that disgusts me. It makes me sick just to think about it.

After I binged, I felt extremely bloated, stuffed, and sick.

I know I'm not in control when I'm bingeing.

I hate to see it—my stomach—like it sticks out. It's rounded, not flat.

Emotionally, I was very angry at myself that I did it again.... I don't like it because I don't want to gain weight. I'm trying to be healthy, and when I do that I'm not being healthy.

The eating part really feels good, it feels good. Afterward I feel like crap, so I get rid of it.... I have to get rid of it because if I don't I'll get fat.

My mood gets worse after I binge. I feel really disgusted with myself for bingeing.... It's not normal. If I didn't get rid of it, I would be so fat. I mean, I'm not thin now, but if I didn't get rid of it, I would be huge.

During the binge, I feel really good. Then I realize that I ate this whole thing and then there is the shame and anger. I realize that I lost control. It is kind of a sinful gluttony...and then I am afraid I am going to gain weight or not lose weight.

I just can't believe it after I binge. I can't believe I'd do something like that. I usually want to kill myself because I feel so desperate and depressed.

I'd rather die than have to live with having binged and not be able to do anything about it.

Why Does She Purge?

Once the distressing thoughts and emotions return, she begins to look for ways to deal with these experiences. She has already binged and her relief was short lived. Now she has to try something else, something that will, she hopes, take care of the intense fear she has of gaining weight. The benefits of the binge are gone, and she is left with the aftermath—the possibility that the binge will lead to weight gain. She has to get rid of that possibility, so she turns to purging.

There are a variety of methods people use to compensate for bingeing. For example:

After I binge, I have to go run. It feels terrible, but if I can go run for an hour or more, I feel like I have made up for it.

The only thing I can think of is to make myself throw up. I know it is gross, but after bingeing I feel so fat and disgusting. I have to do something about it right away.

Throwing up is my usual method of getting rid of the food. I don't trust anything else. I wouldn't know how long I had to exercise to be sure I had done enough. And I can't wait long enough for laxatives or anything to take effect. I have to do something NOW!

The only thing I can think of to do after I eat is to go to the gym and get on one of the machines. Once I'm on it, I get into some kind of a trance, where everything feels calmer, more settled. Nothing else gives me that feeling. I can lose hours being lost in that trance.

I used to just put my finger down my throat. I've been doing it so long that now all I have to do is lean over. I guess that should worry me, but, really, I'm only thinking that I'm glad I can get rid of the food.

I mostly use laxatives. I've heard that they only get rid of water, not what you've eaten. But I don't believe it. I like them because they make me feel like I have been cleaned out—like I can start all over.

I make myself throw up. I do it in the shower so that I can watch everything come up. I try to be as violent as possible. The meaner I can be to myself, the more I feel as if I've been punished for being so stupid. Sometimes I make myself bleed. I guess it's my throat that bleeds; I'm not really sure.

This Is How It Helps

The women we spoke to told us purging was helpful for several reasons. For one thing, like bingeing, it can lessen or eliminate troubling emotions or make them feel numb or invulnerable. Some people compared this purge-induced state to alcohol or drug intoxication. They told us,

> When it is time to purge, it is all I can think about. It is intoxicating. It is like I am in an alcohol-induced stupor. Everything feels numb. I remember getting into a minor accident because I was so anxious to get home to purge.

> I have talked to people who have done crack cocaine. They say that the only time in their lives they feel good about themselves is the few moments they are high on crack. I can relate to that…. I like the feeling I get. It's like a high almost.

> I am so out of it during a purge. I really like that feeling. It seems like nothing can touch me, or at least that I won't care if it does.

Purging is also associated with getting rid of something bad: food. Furthermore, the person with bulimia believes purging wipes out the negative consequences of bingeing—feeling full, fat, weak, lazy, or undisciplined—and it relieves her fear that she will gain weight.

> I felt like I got everything I wanted. I got to eat the hamburger and didn't have to suffer the consequences of gaining weight…. If I kept the food in my body, I would continue to feel full and fat. I mean, I don't like that feeling.

> During the purge, it was like the unique feeling of getting rid of a pimple. That you are getting rid of something that is going to cause harm, that is going to make you fat. You are getting rid of something bad.

> It's great because you get to enjoy eating with only a little guilt in the back of your mind because you know that you are going to throw it up. Then you throw it up and you wipe your face off and you brush your teeth and that's it. You just go on with your day. You're not hungry because you did this to your body and you get rid of the calories.

Yet, for other people, purging is a means of regaining the sense of control they lost by bingeing.

When I purge, I get renewal. Just after I purge, it is like everything is calm and it's all started again. Everything is okay. I clean the toilet, put on my shirt, and it's like my stomach is flat again and I am in control again.

All I know is that I felt better after I purged. I felt less full and more in control. It was a control issue. Hey, I screwed up by eating that second hamburger, but got control back by taking care of it.

I know this sounds strange, but defecating feels good. Purging, I believe, could be closely associated with that same feeling of getting rid of it or control. You couldn't control putting the food inside your body, so you barf and get rid of it.

Finally, purging is associated with feeling good, both emotionally and about one's self. For example,

You know, when I was throwing up a lot I felt like I was doing something really wrong. But when I look back, I do think that I had a lot more confidence.

I actually get excited when I know I will be able to purge.

I have more confidence on the days that I purge. I feel like I am on top of the world, that I can do anything and that no one can stop me.

It Makes Things Better—For Awhile

For some people, the completion of the binge-purge cycle leads to periods of relief. For others, it brings frustration and disappointment. Some things people told us are:

After purging, I feel like I have succeeded.

For me, purging means getting rid of the fattening foods. It makes me feel better. It is, like, instead of alcohol, instead of a shot of tequila, I purge.... It has a calming effect. It gives me confidence. Before I purge, I have all

these negative emotions, and it gives me good emotions instead of the negative ones.... I feel exhausted, but good afterwards.

After I purge, I feel disappointed in myself, really sad and scared. It is like really, really scary because it is so out of control.

I get a break for a while, at least.... Afterwards, the feelings, all the shit comes back.

I feel really disgusted with myself. I look down into the toilet and I think what a horrible thing I did. It's not normal, and so disgusting.... I just feel really disgusted with myself.

Sometimes I'd Rather Just Not Eat

Avoiding weight gain is typically a chief concern of someone with bulimia. Like virtually everyone in our society, she is exposed to intense pressure to be thin. Because she is very concerned about what people think about her and feels insecure about herself as a person, the message that "thin" equals "good" and "fat" equals "bad" especially affects her.

Desperation drives her to purge the food just eaten so it will not cause any weight gain. This desperation also drives her to diet or restrict her food intake between binges. This is done as a way of compensating for bingeing or as a way of avoiding bingeing and purging. If she doesn't binge, she doesn't have to purge. This was common in women we spoke with.

I am so afraid to gain weight from bingeing, so I basically don't eat the rest of the time.

I know I should eat, but I can't. But I know what happens.... I just make myself more hungry, and then I have to binge.

If I binge and purge, then I have to diet the rest of the week.

I'd Rather No One Knew About This

People who have bulimia are generally secretive about their eating behavior. They usually hide their behavior from nearly everyone, especially from those whom they consider to be important or close. With very few exceptions, bingeing and purging takes place in settings where people are alone or where they can take steps to conceal their behavior.

One reason someone with bulimia tries so hard to hide her disorder is that she experiences considerable shame and guilt about bingeing and purging. She feels humiliated because she views her behavior as out of control or as a sign of weakness. She may feel that her loved ones could never understand or forgive her for what she is doing.

Like someone who has anorexia, a person with bulimia very much wants things in her life to look good to the outside world, and for people to respect and think highly of her. The fact that she binges and purges or that she can't stop her behavior is humiliating. And she often feels that her loved ones will think she is disgusting or a bad person if they find out.

Also, for some people bulimia is something they feel they own and that they do not want anyone to take away from them. It's their friend who helps them through the tough times. Keeping it a secret protects the eating disorder. Women told us the following about hiding their disorder:

> *I was very secretive about it, and only did it when nobody was around.*

> *This is not socially acceptable. You can't say to the lady in the bathroom, "Oh, I am sorry, I am going to go in here and throw up. I am bulimic." I mean, it is real secretive, a real private thing, and that is kind of the neat part of it, because it is so private. Nobody knows.*

> *I was real sneaky about hiding my binges. I would cook one tray of brownies for my family and one for myself. That way no one pays attention to how much I eat. They don't know about the other tray.*

> *I don't feel like I have anything in my life. I don't even feel like my life is my own. But my eating disorder is my own. I don't want anyone to take that away from me. They can do whatever else they want, but they can't have my eating disorder.*

I would wake up in the middle of the night and go eat, hoping that my roommates wouldn't hear.

I would never binge in front of anyone. I'd feel like a pig.

The shame of all of this is overwhelming…. I am so weak…The deception, I think, gives me a lot of guilty feelings. I feel guilty that I am deceiving others, because deception is wrong. It is really dishonest to deceive someone like that, especially when they are paying for the food.

I get out of control. I can't stop. I don't want anyone to see me that way.

I have to be alone when I binge. I can't have anyone around me because I would be embarrassed.

I don't tell people about my eating disorder because I don't want them to feel sorry for me. I don't want them to think they need to look at me differently, like, "Oh, that girl has an eating disorder, we better not invite her out to dinner."

The women told us that out of desperation they would often go to great lengths to conceal their bulimia from others. They used a variety of strategies to hide their behavior.

I throw up in little plastic bags and I keep them under my bed. Then, when my mom is gone, I take them out to the garbage. If she found out, I'd die.

I have never thrown up with anyone there. I would do everything I could do to hide it. When I was at home, I would throw up in the shower, because the shower would mask it. When my roommates were home, I would wait until someone started the shower because it masked the noise. In college, I would wait until everyone was out of the bathroom before I would throw up. Sometimes I would be late for class. I always did everything I could so people wouldn't hear.

We were having plumbing problems, so it wasn't a good idea for me to throw up in the toilet. So I started using three-pound coffee cans that I would fill up with vomit and keep in garbage bags, which were kept in the basement until they had to be carried up the stairs and out to the road. This went on for about six months, and when I think of all that vomit fermenting, the things that could have happened as far as something busting loose. It is so scary, yet at the same time, that was a control issue for me. It was like I was getting away with something; I was controlling something and my roommate couldn't do anything about it. I was taking a great deal of risk and I felt that rush, that feeling like I was getting away with something.

I go in my car when I eat. I throw up in there also. That way no one knows I'm doing it. Well, only the people that I drive by while I'm bingeing, I guess, but who cares about them? I'll never see them again.

I make the rounds at fast food restaurants. I try to vary where I go so that the people there don't get to know me. I eat everything and then go throw up somewhere, all before I get home. Then I walk in the door like nothing ever happened. If they only knew.

I'll go buy binge food from the next town over. Everyone in my town knows me now. It is so humiliating. After awhile I'll have to start driving to yet another town. It gets tiring.

I Know It's Not Good For Me, But…

Many girls and women who spoke with us knew that bingeing and purging could lead to bodily damage. This knowledge frightened some of them because the behavior was so strong that they didn't think they could stop it. For others, the need for the disorder was simply too great. Still others knew that their bulimic behaviors were harmful, but they thought that somehow they were invincible to the physical consequences.

I have little cavities in my teeth, which I heard was from purging—the stomach acid.

I recently had a bone density test and it wasn't good. My bones are only as strong as an 80-year-old woman. You'd think that would make me stop, wouldn't you? But I can't.

I am constantly tired, dizzy, and depressed, and I think it is all from my eating disorder.

I think it has ruined my health in a lot of ways. I think it has aged my body a lot, and I feel older than I am.

Well, my teeth, my gums are starting to recede, and my throat is so raw that I think that it's open to infection. Also, I got some ulcers down my throat and it's like a chronic sore throat. My stomach...I can't handle a lot of foods anymore because I know my stomach lining isn't very good, and I know I always blamed it on partying and the tequila I used to drink, but I am sure that throwing up has made my stomach lining yucky.

I feel tired. I am tired all the time, and I get tired quicker. I have really dry skin. I mean, my face gets swollen and there are just physical things. I have had tons of dental work, and now I have just worn the enamel off my teeth. I also have scarring on the back of my hand that won't go away.

I have so messed myself up from all those laxatives, now my body doesn't work right. I guess I should have thought of that before, huh? But I didn't think this would happen to me.

Now I really can't keep anything down. It's funny, I tried for so many years to throw everything up, and now it just happens, even when I don't want it to.

People tell me that I'm ruining my body. I don't believe it. None of those things are going to happen to me. I'm stronger than that.

What Are The Other Ways They Cope?

Bingeing and purging aren't the only methods people use to deal with their distress. Numerous girls and women who talked to us also used other behaviors to cope. Some included drug and alcohol abuse, cutting or burning themselves, working compulsively at school or in a job, and watching enormous amounts of television. They were constantly looking outside themselves for ways to cope with distress. For example,

Home life was a mess. My mom and I fought all the time. I felt trapped in my sad mind and body. So as a way of dealing with it, I began drinking a lot. I started cutting on myself and had a lot of strange sexual experiences. Later, when I was in the teaching program, I was as happy as ever. I was caught up in my business, and I didn't have time to relax. I was going so fast I didn't have time to think or feel.... Even today, I do much better when I keep myself busy, distracted.

I would spend many evenings and weekends at home eating, throwing up, and watching TV.

For some reason, when I did those things, I felt that I had some control. I didn't feel so bad. I didn't feel so down.

When I start to cut or burn, I just go numb. Sometimes I can go numb just thinking about doing it. It feels so still, so calm.

I deal with emotions by keeping busy. I know food is another way I take my mind off whatever I am feeling, but TV, music, exercise, or just running around staying busy would be others. I seem to do a lot better when I have something to do.

When I was doing drugs, I did it like every night for months.... I loved the drugs. I loved everything about them because not only was I thin, I was more confident on them than I have ever been. I wasn't insecure about anything. In fact, insecurity seemed ridiculous. I just felt good all the time.

Hear Their Stories

To help put all this in perspective, we will now tell the stories of two women who suffer from bulimia. Each person and each story is, of course, unique. The experiences of these women, however, are typical of many who suffer from this disorder.

I'm Jeanette

Jeanette is a 21-year-old college junior who suffers from bulimia nervosa. She and her 14-year-old brother grew up in a family with her mother and father. She considers herself to be very close to her family and feels that they have been supportive throughout her life.

Jeanette's mother reports that her daughter has always been very competitive. As early as fourth grade, Jeanette complained to her mother when someone did better than she did in school or at any sort of activity. She enjoys sports and has participated in them on many different levels. She believes her participation in basketball and baseball strengthened her connection with her father, who was her coach for several years.

Jeanette has always made friends easily, but the majority of her friends have been male. She recalls that as early as first grade, her best friend was a boy and that she wasn't particularly interested in having girls as friends. She theorizes that the reason for this was her underlying feeling that she couldn't compete with girls and felt inferior to them. Her athletic abilities and love for sports gave her more in common with boys, and thus facilitated more interactions with them instead of with girls.

Jeanette and her family both confirm that although she has been successful at most things she has attempted, her self-esteem has always been poor and her self-confidence low. She has many self-doubts and feels inferior to most people. Jeanette admits that she dealt with her negative feelings about herself by trying to be as successful as she could in sports and school.

Her adult relationships have been superficial, for the most part, and based almost exclusively on sports or school. Apart from her teammates, she has few friends and has little social interaction other than that related to team activities.

Anxiety often overwhelms Jeanette. She worries about her grades, how well she will play in her next game, and what others think of her. This anxiety pushes her to work extraordinarily hard at whatever activity she is doing.

She has enjoyed many successes, including being a starter in two sports and earning straight A's. Though her social calendar is busy, she admits that most of her friends are actually just acquaintances. She sadly acknowledges that most people really don't know her. She says that if people knew about her eating disorder or constant anxiety, they probably wouldn't believe it. Instead, she believes that most people see her as being highly successful and "together." Jeanette began purging when she was 15 years old. She remembers that she reached puberty the year before and had begun to feel "fatter." In addition, her physical development interfered with her athletic abilities. She felt she could no longer perform at the level she expected to or was used to.

Her first purge occurred after a family meal when someone commented on the amount of food she ate. She remembers feeling instantly fat and tremendously upset because someone else had noticed what she was eating.

Since that moment, anytime she feels fat she purges by vomiting. She admits that purging helps her feel "not as fat" because her stomach looks flatter than it did before the purge. She acknowledges that she binges and purges more often during times of stress, but that no matter what her stress level is, she purges at least once a day.

Here Is How It Worked For Jeanette

Jeanette used her eating disorder as a way to deal with her "overwhelming" emotions, her negative concept of herself, and her inability to initiate and maintain close, emotionally intimate relationships. Her emotions overwhelmed her and she didn't know how to deal with them. When she felt sad, angry, or scared, she experienced distress. She didn't view feelings as a normal part of living. Instead, she saw them as dangerous, as something to avoid. Eating and throwing up was a very effective way to avoid her emotions. During her binges, the anger or sadness that had consumed her just moments before vanished. Instead, she became so focused on eating that nothing else existed.

Jeanette felt negatively about herself and tried to deal with this disparaging self-concept by being as successful as she possibly could be. She received positive attention and validation from her successes, which helped her feel better about herself. Her hope was that by getting enough external validation, her negative thoughts and beliefs about herself would disappear. Unfortunately, any validation she received was temporary; it "didn't stick" and she reverted to feeling badly about herself.

Jeanette also achieved validation by staying thin. She recognized that our society considers thinness attractive and admirable. People's positive comments on her physical size and shape only served to reinforce her belief that "thin is good and fat is bad." Understandably, Jeanette regarded any weight gain a failure. In addition, gaining weight might risk her ability to play sports at the level she wanted, and that would be a tremendous loss to her.

Jeanette relied so heavily on validating herself through the reactions of others that the thought of gaining weight was intolerable. She worried that if she gained weight people wouldn't see her as attractive, and they might also associate her weight gain with other negative characteristics like laziness or selfishness. Her eating disorder was her primary way of coping with the stresses of life.

I'm Callista

Callista went into treatment at age 15. She grew up in a family with a brother and her mother and father. She had always felt close to her family and considered them to be her "best friends." Her brother was three years younger than Callista, and they enjoyed each other's company. Her family traveled quite a bit, something Callista liked.

Callista began making herself throw up at age 13. She wasn't even sure why she did it. "It just seemed like the right thing to do for some reason." She wouldn't have described herself as depressed or upset. She felt she had good friends and that school was going well. Soon, Callista began eating less and making herself throw up more often. Sometimes she would purge three or four times a day. She also began to run several miles each day.

When she was about 14, Callista decided to restrict her food even more. She felt "fat and out of control with my food," and thought that she would feel better if she only ate an apple for breakfast and was "really careful" the rest of the day. Most of the time she threw away her lunch at school and then tried to avoid eating dinner with her family. She also increased her exercise, joining the basketball team at school to "make it look like I was just a normal kid, just wanting to do school sports. But I knew perfectly well that what I was after was burning calories, nothing else. I didn't really even like basketball, but that didn't matter. All that mattered was losing weight."

During this time, she began to binge on large quantities of food. Often, she planned her binges. She thought it was best if she did it when no one was around or after everyone had gone to sleep. There was less chance of getting caught at these times. When she binged, Callista would "eat anything I could find in the house." She often ate the leftovers from dinner, or she made cookies or pies and ate most of what she had cooked. Sometimes she cooked two batches of everything so her family wouldn't realize that she had eaten so much. "I would make two of everything. Then I could eat an entire batch myself and they wouldn't be suspicious, since there would be plenty left for them."

Callista either ate in the kitchen or carried the food to her room where she could eat without anyone knowing. After she had "eaten all I could fit into my stomach," she went into the bathroom, turned on the shower to make noise so her family wouldn't hear her, and made herself throw up. Sometimes she threw up into plastic bags in her room and hid them until she could discard them when no one would notice.

Callista stated that at this point in her life, "All I could think about was bingeing and purging." She didn't hang out with her friends as much anymore. "I couldn't think of anything to talk to them about. I had this big secret life, and what was I supposed to say? 'Hey, guess what I do in my spare time? Eat a lot and make myself throw up!' They would have thought I was crazy. Besides, they were talking about boys and clothes and stuff, and my thoughts were so not on those things. I just didn't care about any of that."

Callista's parents became concerned because she had lost over ten pounds. They were also worried that she seemed so antisocial and that she really didn't talk to them much anymore. They took her to the family physician, who found nothing medically wrong with her, but did suggest that they should watch for the development of an eating disorder. Callista was relieved that she would not have to make any changes in her behavior. She had been worried that the doctor might tell her parents that she couldn't exercise anymore.

Near the end of her freshman year at high school, Callista felt left out and disliked by her friends. She had difficulty concentrating on and finishing her schoolwork. Her grades fell. Callista was disappointed and frustrated with herself. She didn't understand "where things went so wrong." Her life had seemed to be going along so well, and now it was starting to fall apart.

Depression and anxiety were now common. She thought she had everything under control, and now things felt like they were "spiraling out of my control and I didn't know what to do." She continued to binge and purge; she continued to exercise as much as she could. But things only seemed to be getting worse. Then Callista discovered cutting. She couldn't say exactly how she came upon this behavior, but once she found it, she took to it "like a fish to water."

> I liked cutting because I didn't have to deal with eating too much or throwing it up or worrying about gaining weight, and I could hide the cutting. And my parents were totally on my case about eating, anyway. They thought I was getting too skinny and they were threatening to take me back to the doctor.

Callista became "obsessed" with cutting. Though she continued to binge and purge when she could, her main focus was how to get away from people so she could cut. She sometimes looked forward to it all day at school. Needless to say, her friendships continued to decline and she felt more and more left out.

Callista didn't want to kill herself; that was not why she was cutting. She told us, "It gave me that same feeling I had when I purged…like a high, and like nothing could harm me. I felt so okay when I did it. Nothing else mattered. I didn't care about anything." She tried very hard to keep her cutting a secret. Like the bingeing and purging, she didn't think anyone would understand, and that they "would think I was a freak." She did manage to conceal her cutting for several months by cutting mostly on her stomach and upper legs. She also cut her arms, and as long as she wore long-sleeved shirts, no one found out.

However, one morning when Callista hadn't gotten dressed, her mother spotted some of the cuts. Callista was horrified that she had been discovered, and her parents were alarmed that their daughter would do something so harmful. They immediately called their doctor and got the name of a psychotherapist who specialized in treating eating disorders and self-harm.

Here Is How It Worked For Callista

Callista was baffled by why she had started to binge and purge and cut herself. She couldn't come up with any reasons that made sense to her. She realized that most people don't do those things, but her behavior made so much *sense to her,* and she had become very attached to them.

In treatment, Callista began to talk about her life. One of the events she recalled was that an older male relative had molested her when she was 12. At the time, she hadn't thought much about it, believing she had "asked for it" by being alone with him. She thought it "was too late now" to speak up about the incident, but, when speaking with her therapist, she acknowledged that it had been frightening and confusing.

It wasn't long after that event that Callista began to make herself throw up. In therapy, she recognized that bingeing and purging helped her avoid thinking about what had happened with the relative. When she was concentrating on bingeing, throwing up, or what she was going to eat later that day, she was preoccupied. She had no time to think about anything else. She also didn't have to feel her emotions. She felt "high" and invulnerable, as if no harm could come to her.

Callista was ashamed about what her relative did to her and felt that it made her a "bad person." She was afraid to tell anyone for fear that "they wouldn't believe me or would think that I had just asked for it." So Callista suffered in silence, feeling increasingly alone and becoming more isolated from the people around her. Her friends' interests were clothes and boys; she couldn't relate to these things anymore. She was preoccupied with trying not to eat and with overwhelming feelings about being attacked by her relative.

When her parents, concerned by the weight loss, took Callista to see the doctor, she feared that she would be forced to change her behavior. This terrified her. Restricting her food and bingeing and purging had become her coping mechanisms. "I just felt like I would die if they made me stop purging or made me eat more. I didn't know what else to do." The doctor did not try to change anything, much to Callista's relief.

Cutting provided another coping mechanism for her. Cutting herself became yet another way to avoid her distressing thoughts and emotions. Whenever Callista cut herself, she felt "numb, like I was rubber." By cutting, she didn't have to feel the shame, fear, and confusion that ruled her life. Cutting provided an added benefit as far as Callista was concerned. "I got to feel like I was punishing myself. Purging sort of did that too—the more harsh I could be on myself the better. But cutting really did it…. I could see the blood, and the next day it would really hurt." Callista felt she needed to be punished for what had happened with her relative. She hoped that if she could "just punish myself enough that I'd feel better, that it would all go away."

Of course, despite her best attempts, it all didn't go away, and eventually her mother discovered the cutting. However, in treatment Callista began to truly resolve her feelings about being attacked, to understand that it was not her fault and that she wasn't a bad or disgusting person. She also found other ways to cope with emotions and with her life that didn't involve cutting or bulimia. She learned to see her emotions as emotions, not as dangerous or threatening occurrences that might harm her.

Conclusion

Those with bulimia, like Jeanette and Callista, are trapped in a vicious cycle that is extremely difficult to break out of. They become dependent on bingeing and purging as a way of dealing with life. But, like other types of eating disorders, these behaviors can have devastating results, emotionally and physically.

Some girls and women we spoke with remarked about their sadness at how much time had been lost to their bulimia and how having the disorder had altered their lives. At the same time, they acknowledged how important the bulimia had been to them.

> *I don't know what I would have done without it. I don't think I even would have survived. But I also lost so much because of it.*

> *I think, in a way, the eating disorder was a compensation for me not to deal with the real issues in my life. In that sense, it kind of kept me from growing; my growth was retarded. I didn't mature; I didn't deal with those issues. I was stuck. I kept dealing with them through my eating disorder, bingeing and purging…. It has kept me from enjoying all those things I worked so hard to achieve.*

> *I really lost my teenage years and my young adulthood. It is so sad when I think back…all the things I could have been doing, all the friends I could have made, what I could have accomplished…how much fun I could have had.*

The important thing to remember is that your loved one is using her eating disorder as what she perceives to be an effective way of dealing with her negative thoughts, distress emotions, and the anxiety she feels about relationships.

PART III
Embrace Them: Help and Recovery

6

Where Do We Go From Here?
The Treatment for Eating
Disorders

So now what? Your loved one has told you that she has an eating disorder. What next? Who do you call? How do you get her the help she needs?

These are difficult questions, and the answers depend largely on the state of your loved one's eating disorder. Some people with eating disorders need immediate medical care and may require hospitalization, while others might benefit most from outpatient psychotherapy.

The First Step

If your loved one is under 18 years of age, the first step is to make an appointment with her physician. If she is 18 or older, the first step is to strongly, but gently, encourage her to make her own appointment. If she is a minor, you can go with her, but remember to use good judgment about what you say and how you say it. Also, respect the fact that she might feel humiliated by having you in the room with her. If she is an adult, you don't necessarily get to go with her. You can certainly ask. However, remember she may or may not appreciate your support.

As we know, eating disorders are dangerous and can be fatal, so proper medical care is a must. This is true whether or not she looks or feels ill. Remember, a person can have a serious eating disorder and not look particularly ill.

During this appointment, the physician will assess her medical condition. The doctor can be the most helpful if he or she has enough information to make a thorough evaluation. Here are some things the physician will want to know about:

- how long the symptoms have existed and when they first appeared;

- amount of exercise per day, if any;

- is she restricting her food intake (remember: someone with an eating disorder will have a tendency to overestimate the amount of food she is eating);

- if there has been weight loss, how much has been lost, and how fast the weight was lost;

- frequency of bingeing and purging (remember: someone with an eating disorder will have a tendency to underestimate the frequency of purging);

- laxative, diet pill, or diuretic use, or any other chemicals, drugs, medications, or alcohol;

- loss of menstruation;

- dizziness, light-headedness, or fainting; racing or irregular heart beat;

- any other symptoms you may have noticed.

This is a general list and is not exhaustive. What information you provide will, of course, be specific to your loved one's condition. The best rule of thumb is to be as thorough as possible when talking to the physician.

If the physician has experience treating people who have eating disorders, he or she will know what questions to ask. If the physician is not experienced in this area, you should be extra prepared to provide him or her with detailed information about your loved one's eating disorder.

Anorexia and bulimia are extremely complicated, and treating them is an area of specialty. Ideally, your loved one should see a physician who has been trained to deal with these illnesses. It is fine to start with your primary care physician. If this doctor does not have the training or experience to help, he or she will refer you to someone who does.

This first appointment may be quite difficult for your loved one. She may feel exposed, vulnerable, embarrassed, humiliated, or frightened. She may not want to be at the appointment. She might not even think she needs help at this point. Often, she will be angry at whoever made the appointment, and also feel betrayed by this person. Here are some things people have told us.

> *I couldn't believe they made me go. I felt like if they really loved me, they wouldn't make me do it. I hated them at first. I couldn't believe it was for my own good.*

> *I was SO scared. I didn't know what was going to happen. I thought it might be something bad and harmful. My mom didn't know what was going to happen either, so she couldn't help me be less scared.*

> *I didn't know what to say to the doctor. She asked me all kinds of questions, but it didn't make any sense to me. I didn't think anything was wrong. I didn't think I needed to be there.*

> *I was so mad. The doctor asked me if I was purging, and I said no. Then my mother told him that she knew I was throwing up. I couldn't believe she said that. It wasn't until months later that I forgave her and could see that she was only trying to help so he would know the truth.*

Remember how threatened people with eating disorders can be if they feel someone is trying to take away their disorder. Being aware of this can help you and your loved one get through this initial appointment.

It is also useful to remember how difficult it can be for someone with anorexia or bulimia to know how to describe what is going on with her. As we have said earlier in the book, someone with an eating disorder may not be able to identify physical symptoms, and she may not be aware of her emotions. Sometimes family members make the mistake of interpreting her difficulty in speaking about symptoms as "just being bratty" or "resistant" or "stubborn." In some cases this is correct, but many times she actually feels like she is in the dark about what is happening.

People have told us that the responses they received from the medical community have been wide ranging, from tremendously helpful to completely insensitive. For example, consider these comments.

The medical assistant told me as she was weighing me that I didn't look anorexic. As soon as she said that to me, I knew I wasn't going to eat that day.

I sat there while the doctor told me that I was selfish and that I was putting my parents through hell. I thought to myself "Yeah, dumb ass, I wake up every morning thinking how great it is to be anorexic."

The doctor was so great. She was nice and seemed to know exactly what to say. I was really scared going the first time, but she made me feel less afraid.

He just looked at me and asked why I was there. I told him that I had bulimia, and he just looked at me and said, "What do you think I can do about that?" I felt like an idiot, like I should've never gone and that I was wasting his time.

It actually turned out to be a relief. The doctor knew what he was talking about, and I could ask him tons of questions. He didn't make fun of me like I thought he was going to. I ended up not feeling so alone.

The doctor said to me, "Why don't you just binge on carrots? They don't have any calories, so you wouldn't have to throw up." I was thinking...he so does not get this at all. I'm not ever going to tell him anything.

I didn't want to go, but once I was there it seemed like an okay idea. The doctor had worked with a lot of girls like me, and she could tell me what was going on with my body. I had been feeling so strange for months, but I didn't know it was because of how I was eating. She explained how not eating enough affects my body. I'm not sure if I'll be able to change anything right away, but at least I understand better what is happening.

After this initial medical evaluation, what's next? The next step depends on your loved one's condition and the severity of her eating disorder. There are several levels of care for treating eating disorders. We'll describe each of them and tell you how to figure out what level of care might be appropriate.

Levels Of Care

Outpatient Treatment

The least intensive level of care is outpatient treatment. This type of treatment is appropriate for people who are medically stable (those who do not need emergency medical care or to be in a medical hospital with 24-hour medical care), and for people who are generally functioning well in their lives. By this we mean those who do not need high levels of supervision with regard to the eating disorder and feel like they have some control over their disorder, particularly when it comes to eating, purging, or exercise behavior.

Most people who are diagnosed with an eating disorder begin treatment at this level. An outpatient treatment plan generally consists of a team of professionals who have different areas of expertise and who work together to stabilize the disorder and help your loved one begin to recover.

The basic professionals on an outpatient treatment team are a psychotherapist (this can be a psychologist, social worker, or master's-level therapist); a medical doctor; and a dietitian.

We talked about the initial job of the physician earlier in this chapter. The medical doctor also has an ongoing role to play, and that is to monitor the patient to make sure she remains medically stable. The physician will routinely check things such as heart rate, blood pressure, potassium, and other electrolyte levels. The more serious the eating disorder, the more closely her doctor will want to monitor her health. Regardless of your loved one's level of care, make sure she is being monitored by a physician.

The job of the psychotherapist is to help the person begin to understand and then work through the issues that are fueling her eating disorder. Together they must figure out how the eating disorder functions in her life and then develop healthier coping skills so she doesn't need to rely on her eating disorder.

The psychotherapist's primary role is to help your loved one understand her distress (emotions or relationships, for example), and to see how her disorder has tried to protect her from these experiences. It is also the job of the psychotherapist to help her learn to deal with these things without using the eating disorder as an aid. These can be difficult and time-consuming tasks, but they are imperative for recovery.

The role of the dietitian initially is to help stabilize her nutritionally. People with eating disorders often know a great deal about nutrition (for instance, for a particular food, they will know the calorie content, the fat content, and the percentage of carbohydrates), but they have a very difficult time putting this knowledge into action when it comes to themselves.

In fact, they tend to use that knowledge against themselves much of the time. For instance, a patient recently told us, "I've heard that Americans eat way too much fat, so I'm just being healthy." This person misinterpreted for whom that statement was intended (it wasn't meant for her), and therefore cut all fat from her diet. Someone else said, "I've read that too much protein isn't good for you" (so this person severely restricted her protein intake, putting her health at risk).

The dietitian can develop a nutritional plan that meets your loved one's needs and begins to stabilize her body. The dietitian then helps to confront myths and misunderstandings the person may have about food and nutrition. As recovery progresses, the dietitian helps her reintroduce foods that she has considered "unsafe" and has been afraid to eat. An eventual nutritional goal is for her to be able to listen to what her body needs and to base her eating on that instead of what the eating disorder tells her she should do (for example, by judging whether body size is all right by what the numbers on the scale may say or by how few calories she can eat in a day).

Depending on your loved one's situation, family therapy may be indicated. Family therapists work with others in the family, in addition to the person who has the eating disorder. An eating disorder affects the entire family, and we have found that everyone can benefit from help and support. Here are a few things parents have told us.

> *We were so afraid. We thought we were to blame for her illness and that we had ruined her in some way. We needed a lot of help to understand that the way our family worked, or didn't work, did have a part in why she had gotten sick, but it wasn't that we had set out to harm her—or that we meant for this to happen.*

> *She always had worried about out marriage. We tried to convince her that things were okay, but she still worried. It was like she was trying to take care of us and make sure we were okay. We all had to figure out different ways of being together.*

> *Her mother had such difficulty expressing herself. And I am a pretty open person…. We have very different ways of dealing with the world. These differences affected our daughter more than we had realized. We never imagined they might have something to do with her eating disorder.*

> *There was a lot of competition between her and her sisters. We never understood that…. All three of them are such terrific girls. And we didn't see it, that it had to do with us in any way. We all had to learn to understand what this competitive stuff meant in our family and then to deal with that. It was tough, but we are glad that we did it. It has given our whole family a lot more freedom, and we are a lot closer now.*

Finally, group therapy may be of value to your loved one. People with anorexia and bulimia often feel alone and like there are no other people going through what they are going through. Being in a group with others who also have eating disorders provides a place to feel connected to other people, to see that they are not alone or "a freak," and to relate to people who are suffering in similar ways as they are.

Intensive Outpatient Programs

The next higher (more intensive) level of care is an intensive outpatient program. This is typically at least three hours of structured treatment per day, and all of the providers are typically at the same location. This is a good choice if your loved one has tried an outpatient treatment plan and found that it doesn't quite provide enough support or structure for her to make changes in her eating behavior.

These programs can either replace or be combined with a traditional out-patient treatment plan. They usually provide some combination of individual and family psychotherapy, group therapy, groups to help educate families about eating disorders, and nutritional counseling. The treatment team typically consist of a psychotherapist, a family therapist, a medical doctor, and a dietitian.

Patients participating in intensive outpatient programs need to be medically stable because these programs typically do not provide intensive medical supervision (usually people continue to be followed by their regular physician during the time they are in the program).

Day-Treatment

A more comprehensive level of care is a day-treatment program (sometimes also called a partial hospitalization program). A day-treatment program offers full-day support, typically six to eight hours per day, at the end of which the patient goes home. This allows the patient to be part of her family or home life in the evening, while participating in highly structured treatment during the day. A day-treatment program offers even more structure and support than an intensive outpatient program.

Day-treatment programs usually offer therapy groups during most of the day, as well as several meals. Individual therapy, nutritional counseling, and sometimes a family component are typically included. If you are investigating a day-treatment program, be sure it is designed for eating disorders. There are many kinds of day-treatment programs, and it would not be appropriate to choose one that wasn't equipped to help your loved one with her eating disorder.

The day-treatment approach has significant advantages. First, it allows the patient to practice what she learns in the program when she goes home at night and on weekends. It is one thing to learn new ways of being in the world, and a whole other thing to be able to use them in one's daily life without reverting back to the old, eating-disordered ways.

For someone considering going to an inpatient or residential eating disorders program (which we will talk about next), the second advantage of partial and day-treatment programs is the cost. These programs offer a very high degree of supervision and support, but they are a fraction of the cost of inpatient treatment.

Inpatient or Residential Treatment

Inpatient or residential treatment is where your loved one lives at the treatment facility full time. These programs are for those who do not need acute medical care, but require 24-hour supervision and structure.

This environment is best for those who cannot gain weight by themselves, or have not been able to alter their eating-disordered behavior in an outpatient setting, or need supervision at and after all meals.

This method of treatment removes your loved one from the family, which for many is very difficult. For others, this level of treatment provides an opportunity to focus on fighting their eating disorder without the distraction of their day-to-day lives. This is also a good treatment environment for those who are resistant to treatment or who feel that their eating disorder controls them completely.

Medical Hospitalization

The most acute level of care for those suffering from eating disorders is inpatient medical hospitalization. Typically, medical hospitalizations are advised when your loved one's physical health is compromised and she needs immediate medical care. In this case, the hospitalization is relatively short term, with the focus being on rehydration, refeeding, and medical stabilization. As we mentioned earlier in the book, eating disorders are physically taxing and potentially life threatening. That is why it is imperative for a physician to monitor your loved one.

Choosing Someone To Help

When looking for professionals to treat your loved one, you need to ask many questions. Do not be shy! Oftentimes, loved ones feel so desperate to find help that they settle for the first person who has said they've worked with people who have eating disorders. As we said at the beginning of this chapter, treating people with anorexia, bulimia, or binge eating is difficult and very specialized. Make sure that the person who is going to be treating your loved one has adequate experience and knowledge about eating disorders. Some questions you might want to ask are:

- What is your philosophy about what causes an eating disorder and how someone recovers from one? (Not all professionals have the same beliefs about eating disorders; it is important your loved one works with people she feels have views she can relate to and feel comfortable with.)

- Do you have other professionals with whom you work? How long have you collaborated with them? How do you feel about working with other professionals? Is working as a member of a treatment team the typical way that you work with people with eating disorders, or do you generally work in some other way?

- How long have you treated people with eating disorders?

- What specialized training have you had?

- What percentage of people with whom you work have eating disorders?

- What resources would you use if my loved one requires a higher level of care?

Rely on people you trust, such as your loved one's physician or someone you know who has recovered from an eating disorder. That person may know where to direct you to begin to look for help.

7

What Should We Expect?
The Phases of Treatment

There are several phases of treatment and recovery, and each one has different challenges, as well as rewards. In this chapter, we describe these stages, help you understand what goes on in each of them, and give you some idea of what to expect along the way. We also follow two women through the recovery process so you can see how this all fits together.

It's important to keep in mind that these phases are very general. As we have said, each person has her own path of recovery. However, in our experience, most people go through some version of these stages. Also, keep in mind that recovery is not a straight line; sometimes it can seem like a person takes one step forward and two steps back. Family members and other loved ones often worry when this happens, fearing it means she isn't progressing in treatment. But ups and downs are a normal part of recovering from an eating disorder. What is important is her overall trend toward getting better.

It is also normal for her recovery to proceed at different speeds at different points, for her to have less difficult periods and more difficult periods, and for her to have times where she feels hopeful and times where she is terribly frustrated or even wants to give up.

Recovery from anorexia or bulimia can be very difficult. She will need help maintaining the perspective that things can get better, and this is where you can be of great value to her.

Phase One: Stabilization

The first phase begins when she enters treatment. The focus of this period of treatment is on containing and stabilizing her eating disorder. The aim of treatment at this phase is to stop the progression of the disorder; in other words, to prevent her condition from getting worse. The second goal is to begin to turn the course of the disorder around. Several areas of stabilization need to be addressed: medical, psychological, behavioral, and nutritional.

Medical Stabilization

It is difficult, and sometimes impossible, to do any of the psychological work necessary to directly address the eating disorder if someone is significantly underweight, is severely malnourished, or is experiencing medical complications caused by her eating disorder. She simply will not be able to think or feel clearly enough. If she enters treatment in this state, most of the first phase of treatment will focus on helping her improve her physical condition and to begin to get to a stable weight where she can think clearly.

For someone who has anorexia and is severely underweight and/or medically compromised, medical stabilization is achieved when she has gained enough weight that she is out of acute medical danger and her lab results (electrolyte levels) are stable.

An individual with bulimia has accomplished medical stability for phase one when her lab results are consistently within normal range and when her purging is infrequent enough that it doesn't cause her to become seriously dehydrated or her electrolytes to become unbalanced.

Becoming medically stable does not mean that the person is totally out of the woods or that she will never be in acute medical danger again during the course of her disorder. As we have said before, recovery is not a straight line; she may have difficulties at other points along the way. However, if she can get through the initial difficulties and challenges of becoming more stable medically and nutritionally, it is a good sign.

Psychological Stabilization

Depression and anxiety are common in anorexia and bulimia, and they can make it difficult and sometimes impossible for the person to function in her life. When these conditions interfere with her ability to focus on or understand treatment, stabilization must be an immediate goal. One thing that psychological stabilization means is that these concerns have been addressed and are in the process of being resolved.

Depression and anxiety may be addressed in various ways; sometimes the relief of having found people to help her and knowing that she is now on a path toward recovery can alleviate some of the hopeless feelings she may have. Medication can also be quite valuable for some people who are depressed or anxious.

Another criterion for psychological stabilization is that the eating-disordered thinking and behaviors do not have such a tight grip on her. Anorexia and bulimia can consume a person's thought process; sometimes there is little room for anything else.

Her treatment team will help her become more aware of her eating disorder thoughts and different ways of responding to them. Doing this will begin to loosen the grip the disorder has on her. She will also need help remembering that there are other things in life besides her disorder, and that it is okay for her to think about other things.

Behavioral Stabilization

The behavior of someone who is restricting or bingeing and purging often can be so out of control that it takes up a lot of her time. It also can totally exhaust her. In this case, part of the first phase of treatment focuses on reigning in these behaviors so she can get a clearer sense of what is happening to her and an idea of what is triggering her behavior.

Her treatment team will help her obtain basic insight into the meaning of her eating-disordered behavior and the purpose that is serves in her life. In addition, they will begin to help her develop alternatives to these behaviors. As she begins to see that her behavior is more about dealing with her personal distress than managing her weight, she can make use of alternative coping skills.

She now begins to have a choice. She can use her eating-disordered behavior to deal with a given situation, or she can try some other strategy she has developed. This isn't the complete answer to her eating disorder, but it is a first step in halting the behavioral progression so the underlying issues causing the eating disorder can be identified and addressed.

Practical skills for talking to family members, co-workers, or friends, or dealing with other relationships, can also be of great value at this point. For example, people often tell us that they don't know what to say to a family member about her eating disorder or the fact that she has begun treatment. They may need assistance in discovering new ways to communicate.

Nutritional Stabilization

The initial nutritional goal of this first phase is to get her to eat a consistent amount of food. She needs to provide her body with enough nutrients to function normally. Someone with anorexia needs help to begin to eat enough food. Women with bulimia need help stabilizing their erratic eating patterns.

To accomplish this goal, she may be put on a meal plan and have her caloric intake monitored. A dietitian must monitor the process of nutritional stabilization because there are many complexities in dealing with someone who is used to starving herself or bingeing and/or purging.

Her nutritional status and the quantity that she has been able to eat recently will determine where she and her dietitian start this process. The two of them may need to start slowly and gradually make changes in her food intake. This strategy gives her body a chance to get used to the adjustments. It also offers her an opportunity to deal with the anxiety that eating differently than she has become accustomed to may cause.

Yes, There Is Hope

A final goal of this phase is to provide hope about recovery. Many times, a person comes to us feeling discouraged or hopeless about her situation. She may not think she has the strength or ability to change her eating disorder. Her loved ones may be worried about this also. The treatment team must help everyone involved to understand that, although it will be hard work and will take some time, recovery is possible and she can succeed.

How Long Does the First Phase Of Treatment Take?

This first phase of treatment can last a few weeks to several months—or longer. How long it takes depends on how medically, nutritionally, and psychologically ill the person is when she begins treatment. In addition, how strong her support system is and how well she can make use of treatment will affect her capacity to make these first changes in her eating disorder.

In this first stage of treatment, your loved one will meet and begin working with the basic members of her treatment team. The specific team members and the level of care may be adjusted at later points during the course of treatment, but the main components will be established at this time.

Having achieved some stability, she will be able to make much better use of the psychotherapeutic part of treatment. She will not feel so much as if she is living in a fog anymore; her thinking will be much clearer, and she will feel more "in touch" with her emotions and with what is happening to her.

What's It Like For My Loved One?

It has been our experience that people are very frightened during this phase of treatment and recovery. They often feel extremely out of control, and sometimes they are embarrassed or humiliated by their behavior. They can also feel threatened by entering treatment. Even someone who *wants* to recover can be conflicted and ambivalent about treatment and what might happen if she tries to change her disorder.

Many times, people are afraid that they won't exist without their eating disorders or that they will not be able to manage in life. In this first phase of treatment, people often feel the need to cling desperately to the disorder and therefore may resist stabilization.

Understanding your loved one's fears about changing or resolving her disorder can help both you and her. Sometimes family members have said things to us like, "We are just trying to help her. Why is she so resistant?" or "She acts like we are going to hurt her. What is she so afraid of?" or "She is just so stubborn. She doesn't want help" or "Why can't someone fix her?"

The person who has the disorder is usually terrified, and her extreme fear can manifest as stubbornness, rebelliousness, or anger. She may not be able to identify what it is about beginning treatment that's so frightening for her. You can help by listening carefully to her and remembering that fear may be a big part of what she is experiencing. Also, remember how difficult it can be for someone with anorexia or bulimia to figure out what she is feeling and that even when she *does* know, consider how hard she finds it to express her experience to others.

Now we'll get to know Karen and Mariko. We will meet each one as she begins phase one of treatment for an eating disorder, then we'll join up with them later as they go through phases two and three of their journey to recovery.

Karen's Journey

Karen had been anorexic for about four years. The eating disorder began just before her junior year in high school. Her parents had been concerned about her for some time, but Karen insisted that she was fine. Several times, Karen's parents took her to their family physician, but each time the doctor told them, "This will pass. It's a phase that lots of girls go through."

She was a few months into her second year at a university when she finally began treatment for the anorexia. During the first two months of her sophomore year at college, Karen's parents had seen her weight drop significantly. Her grades were good, but she wasn't having any fun at school and everything was extremely difficult for her. There were many family arguments about what to do; Karen's parents wanted her to take some time off from school to get healthier, but Karen was against that idea. When she fainted on her way to class one day, the decision was made.

Karen agreed to be evaluated at an inpatient eating disorders program. Her parents came with her, and she met with a therapist, a nutritionist, a medical doctor, and a psychiatris, who all agreed that Karen needed to be admitted right away. She was given a full physical exam, including blood work, which showed that she was severely dehydrated and that her potassium level was dangerously low. She needed immediate care.

Karen was terrified. She thought that her school would throw her out and that her life would be ruined. She was even more afraid that being in treatment meant she would have to eat, and that seemed like the end of the world to her.

Karen was admitted to the program and put on an IV to stabilize her potassium and to rehydrate her. She needed to be on bed rest for several days to ensure her medical safety. After four days, Karen's blood work was stable, and she was able to begin participating fully in the program.

Throughout her first weeks in the program, Karen maintained that nothing was wrong and that she didn't need to be there. She was constantly angry, particularly with her parents for making her stay in the program. Karen struggled greatly with eating, sometimes having to rely on a liquid supplement to meet her nutritional needs.

As the weeks progressed, Karen was able to eat more and more solid food, although her anxiety about eating and "getting fat" remained high. She also began to feel depressed. This was not unexpected, as the anorexia had concealed her emotions. Only when she began to get more nutritionally stable did her emotions began to emerge.

Beginning to feel again was very distressing for Karen. She so wanted to return to starving herself, which she acknowledged made her "feel much safer" and in control. In the therapy groups that filled her days in the program, Karen was encouraged to discuss her fears about having emotions and to begin to identify what her anorexia meant to her.

Karen's parents also participated in treatment while she was in the program. They came weekly for family meetings with Karen and her therapists. They also attended groups with other parents so they could get support and talk with other people in similar situations.

Karen remained in the eating disorders program for about ten weeks. For her, this ten weeks was phase one of treatment. She managed to gain enough weight so she was no longer in medical danger. Her lab results remained stable. She was still very frightened about continuing to eat, but, because she could think clearer now that she was far less malnourished, she was able to reason with herself about how important it was to continue with treatment and with her eating.

When she was ready to leave the hospital, Karen was referred to an outpatient therapist, a dietitian, and a physician to continue her work in recovery. She was now ready for phase two, which focused on identifying, understanding, and resolving the issues that fueled the eating disorder—issues such as emotions, relationships, and self-concept, which Karen found frightening and difficult.

Mariko's Journey

Mariko had suffered from bulimia since she was 15, and she entered treatment at age 25. She had managed to keep her eating disorder a secret from everyone she knew, including her entire family and her fiancé. She had "felt too humiliated to get help" until now, but believed that she "couldn't go on like this" anymore.

Although she had a full-time job, two parents, a younger sister, and a fiancé whom she loved, Mariko's life revolved around bingeing and purging. On a typical day, she might binge and purge three to five times. Most of the time, she felt exhausted and weak.

Mariko told her fiancé that she needed help, and together they went to a psychologist who specialized in treating eating disorders. The therapist referred her also to a dietitian and a medical doctor. Mariko saw both of these clinicians within the next few weeks. The physician performed extensive blood work and an EKG to make sure Mariko's heart was stable. Her lab results were on the low side of normal and her blood pressure was low, but not dangerously so. The EKG showed nothing abnormal. The dietitian assessed Mariko's nutritional status and then formulated a nutritional plan to begin stabilizing her diet.

Although she felt humiliated by having bulimia, Mariko was relieved to be getting help. "For the first time in years, I felt like there might be hope for me to get better." Mariko continued with treatment consistently for the next six weeks. She worked very hard to follow her treatment team's advice, but she found it extremely difficult to make any changes in her bingeing and purging behavior. She had "been doing it so long that I couldn't imagine how to stop."

One week her blood work came back abnormal. She was dehydrated and her electrolyte levels were off. Most alarming was that her potassium was significantly low. This concerned her treatment team because it meant that Mariko was at greater risk for medical complications, including cardiac arrest. Her physician sent her to the emergency room to be hydrated and to get her electrolyte levels back within normal range.

Within a few days, Mariko's lab results were off again. Her bingeing and purging kept throwing her body off, and she was unable to maintain her blood levels, despite having been rehydrated at the hospital. Her physician felt that Mariko was in sufficient medical danger to warrant being admitted into a hospital.

Although unhappy about it, Mariko agreed to be admitted to a medical unit. She stayed in the hospital for five days. The doctors and nurses there worked to help her eat consistently and to resist purging. It was very difficult for her, but having staff with her 24 hours each day gave her a lot of structure and support that made things a little easier.

Mariko was considerably more stable when she left the hospital. She had now had practice eating without purging, she was well hydrated, and her electrolytes were within normal range. She felt ready to continue her work outside the hospital.

Over the next few months, Mariko managed to keep her purging to less than twice a day. This made her feel better about her life and her ability to recover. It also helped keep her from getting dehydrated and having her electrolyte levels become unstable.

Phase one for Mariko meant reducing her bingeing and purging enough to allow her blood levels to stay out of a dangerous zone. She still binged and purged, but she felt that she had greater control over the behavior and that she wasn't "spending all day thinking about my next binge."

Phase Two: Exploring

In phase two, the bulk of the psychological and behavioral work takes place. By now, your loved one has gotten herself significantly more stable, and the main focus of treatment is no longer on crisis management and acute concerns about medical complications. Now that she is stronger and able to think more clearly, she could make better use of treatment.

Psychological and emotional goals in this phase include understanding how the eating disorder functions in her life, identifying and resolving issues that underlie the disorder and continuing to figure out healthier ways to cope with her life so she doesn't need to rely on the eating disorder as a way of dealing with things.

As far as behavioral goals, for someone who is underweight an important focus of this phase is continuing to increase her weight into an acceptable range. Regaining weight is usually very difficult and presents many challenges. It is also important to remember that this process is not linear; sometimes she will progress steadily and sometimes she may falter. The overall pattern of what her weight does is what's most important.

For someone who binges and/or purges, a goal in this phase of treatment is to understand those behaviors and their purposes, as well as to make significant reductions in the frequency that they occur.

In this phase of treatment, as in phase one, treatment is often a central focus of someone's life. We often tell people that recovering from an eating disorder is a full-time job. Treatment and recovery require an enormous amount of energy and commitment, and, like having a full-time job, they can be quite tiring. Sometimes it is difficult or impossible for someone to hold a job or go to school during this time.

Let's rejoin the two women we met in phase one and see what phase two looks like for them.

Back to Karen

Karen did very well in the inpatient eating disorders program. She had gotten used to the structure there and learned to feel reasonably comfortable about eating in that situation. By the time she was discharged, her weight had stabilized and she was not in medical danger. She was, however, still significantly underweight.

The first few weeks out of the program were difficult. Though she and the program had set up an outpatient plan for her, she would be in treatment only a few hours per week, not all day long, as before.

The transition from an inpatient program to an outpatient treatment plan is often quite difficult. Like Karen, many people learn to feel safe while in an inpatient program due to the intensive structure that setting provides. Adjusting to things such as cooking and shopping for food, scheduling appointments, having free time, and interacting with family and friends can be frightening.

Sometimes people struggle with food and eating during this adjustment. This is fairly typical, and it's important to be prepared in case it happens. Generally, as someone gets used to her new treatment team and life outside an eating disorders program, things settle down.

Karen liked her new treatment team, which consisted of a therapist, a dietitian, and a physician. She saw each of them two times a week, the plan being to reduce the number of visits as Karen became increasingly healthier. Every few weeks, her parents also went to see the therapist, sometimes with Karen and sometimes just by themselves so they could get the support they needed, ask any questions they had, and feel secure in how they were dealing with Karen's illness.

In therapy, Karen talked about what she had learned in the eating disorders program, what she thought about her anorexia, and what she might want to change in her life. It became clear to her that she was very afraid of living without the illness. She worried that she "wouldn't know what to do, that I'll be lost without it and just flail around in my life." Karen felt that "everyone else knows what to do with themselves. They aren't afraid like I am. They have some plan for themselves that they can rely on." She had come to rely on the anorexia for security and structure in her life.

Over the next few months, as she continued to look back on her life, Karen became increasingly aware that she had always felt "lost and like I didn't know what I was doing. It didn't matter what anyone said to me, like, 'don't worry, you are doing fine' or 'everything is okay, just calm down.' I just panicked all the time that I was about to fall apart." She could see clearly that the anorexia had developed as a way to help her better deal with her negative self-concept and distressing emotions and to "hold things together."

Karen also began to talk about the difficulties her parents had and her feeling that their marriage "was not really good at all." She thought that her mother and father loved each other but that they "had so many problems communicating and they were such different people, I don't see how they even stayed together."

She talked about how her parents' relationship affected her and how their difficulties may have influenced how she felt about herself. "Now that I look back, I sometimes wish they wouldn't have stayed together. I know they did it for me because they thought it would be the best for me, but I'm not sure now. Watching them all these years has made me doubt relationships and feel like I shouldn't get married. Like it would never work."

Karen felt "wrong" talking about her parents, and she felt guilty saying she thought the family had problems. She also began to realize that she had "never been able to tell the truth about my family. I always thought I could only say *nice* things, and that this might have been one of the reasons the anorexia developed." She shared,

> I felt such pressure to always make everything look pretty. To make it look like we had the best family ever. In a lot of ways it was really good, and I'm grateful for that. I love my parents. And I know they love me. But we weren't…we aren't perfect. So I felt like I was lying a lot. And I hated that. Maybe part of the way I dealt with the pressure was by not eating.

She also thought that growing up in a family where she worried about the stability of her parents' marriage left her feeling insecure and "on edge" about life, that it made her feel "things were always precarious, that maybe they would just disappear suddenly. I worried a lot that my parents would just out of the blue say they were getting divorced. And then what would I have done? I was so afraid of that. All the time."

Although it was difficult, Karen felt that her therapy was going well and she was making progress in gaining the weight that she needed to, but the eating and weight gain were very difficult. Many days she didn't want to eat at all, and it was a struggle just to get through the day. Some weeks her weight would continue to rise, and other times she would have lost some weight.

One of the most difficult things for Karen was the fact that she couldn't exercise.

> *I had always been so active, and now they were telling me I couldn't even go swimming or to the gym. They didn't even want me climbing too many stairs. I couldn't believe they thought going up some stairs was exercise.*

While she was in the program, Karen had been closely monitored, so it was easier for her to keep track of her activity level. When she was out of the program, she had to be in charge of how active she was.

> *It was a constant battle for me. The anorexia kept saying, "You are SO fat and you need to go running," but then there was another part of me that said, "No, you need to get stronger before you can do that." All in all, it was a nightmare. I don't even think anyone knew how hard it was. After all, they couldn't know what I was going through. They couldn't read my mind or anything, and I couldn't really explain it to them.*

Several months had now passed since Karen's discharge from the inpatient program. She was still seeing her therapist twice a week, but she had cut back seeing the dietitian and the doctor to once a week. This seemed to work well, and Karen felt she had adequate support from her treatment team. Her parents continued to go to their therapist about every six weeks.

In general, Karen liked the fact that she was getting stronger, both physically and emotionally, but she was also afraid. She felt like she still needed the anorexia to help her deal with her life, and she remained uncertain that she could manage without it. At one point, about eight months after getting out of the inpatient program, her fears became particularly intense.

> *I just felt I was getting so much closer to not having the anorexia. And while I was glad in some ways, I was also terrified. Actually, I really missed the disorder. I know it sounds weird, but it is true. Things were so clear and safe when I was really in it.*

Not surprisingly, Karen's weight began to drop. Her treatment team helped Karen and her family understand the reasons behind the sudden turn in her weight. As Karen continued to deal with her fears about living without the anorexia, her eating began to stabilize again.

It took about a year and a half from when she was discharged from the hospital for Karen to reach a goal weight range, and this eighteen months was phase two of her treatment and recovery. Her menstrual cycle returned, and she felt much stronger and healthier than she had in many years. Still, eating was difficult at times and she "sometimes felt fat." Despite this, she was able to maintain her weight in an appropriate range and add some exercise without it negatively affecting her health.

By this time, Karen had developed a thorough understanding of what the anorexia meant to her and how it functioned in her life. She began to more directly deal with her emotions, negative self-concept, and relationships which she found distressing. Her family also had grown to understand the disorder, and they knew how they could support Karen's continued recovery. Karen still needed some help, but she was now ready for the third phase of treatment and recovery.

Back to Mariko

Mariko had been out of the medical hospital for several months now. She continued her treatment and began to feel that she might be able to recover from her bulimia. She was still bingeing and purging at least once a day, and often two times a day. In general, though, she was able to stabilize her eating so that she was taking in an adequate amount of nutrition each day. Mariko's blood levels were staying stable from week to week at this point, which was reassuring to her and to her treatment team.

She and her therapist were working on the issues that Mariko thought might have triggered the development of her eating disorder. She divulged, for the first time, that when she was 15 she had been on a first date with a boy, and he had attacked her and raped her. She had been terrified and had tried to escape, but he was much bigger than she, and he forced her to have sex with him. Mariko had never told anyone about this before. She thought that it was somehow her fault, that she "should have been able to stop it, or should have seen it coming or something."

Mariko was able to connect this event with the onset of her bulimia. For the first time, she was able to talk about her fear, disgust, and feelings of hopelessness and helplessness. Her therapist helped her understand that the attack had not been her fault and that she had done everything she could to get away from the boy; he had simply been too big for her to escape from him. Mariko was relieved to finally tell the truth about the rape. However, talking about it and feeling the emotions she had so long avoided was powerful. She began to binge and purge more frequently.

Mariko wondered if she wasn't "just getting worse," because her symptoms seemed to increase. At times, her family wondered about this also. But Mariko made the connection between the intensity of emotions she was dealing with and her need to binge and purge. She understood that the bingeing and purging were ways that helped her feel less flooded by her emotions.

She began to deal with and understand her emotions, and she was much better able to talk about what had happened to her. It is fairly typical in the treatment of an eating disorder for someone's symptoms to become more intense at times, as she works through the issues that underlie her disorder. As a family member, it can be very helpful and reassuring to remember this, but sometimes her symptoms worsening is not a sign that things are getting better. It is important for the person with the disorder and her treatment team to be aware of the difference and know what to do in either case.

Although it was difficult, Mariko continued to work on the attack and many related issues. She began to see why it was difficult for her to trust her fiancé and why she had such strong feelings of "always being on guard, always ready to either fight or run."

As she really came to terms with what had happened, Mariko became seriously depressed. Letting herself talk about the attack had opened up "a Pandora's box of emotions for me, and I didn't feel like I could cope with it all." About a year into treatment, Mariko felt suicidal. She was able to talk openly with her therapist about this, and together they strategized about how to handle the situation.

One of the things they decided to do was have Mariko see a psychiatrist and discuss medication. They both knew that medication wouldn't solve everything but that it might help her with her increasing depression. Her depression had gotten so severe that she had difficulty getting up in the morning and difficulty concentrating in therapy and elsewhere in her life. She maintained her job, but it took "all I had just to hold it together."

Mariko saw a psychiatrist, who agreed that medication might be helpful. She began an antidepressant and made another appointment with the psychiatrist for follow-up. As the medication began to take effect, Mariko felt better able to cope with her life. She could focus on continuing her recovery.

With the help of her treatment team, family, and friends, Mariko was able to fully come to terms with having been raped. As she worked through the emotions, thoughts, and beliefs related to that trauma and understood their connection to her bulimia, Mariko was able to decrease her bingeing and purging. It wasn't always easy; she found herself being pulled to binge often, but she was increasingly able to find other ways of dealing with her feelings.

On the average, Mariko binged and purged two times per week, a significant reduction from when she had begun treatment. She felt committed to further reducing the frequency of her bingeing and purging, but she was proud of the fact that after nine years of bingeing and purging three to five times per day, she had been able to get it down to twice a week.

For Mariko, phase two lasted about two years. It ended when she felt the issues that fueled the bulimia had been thoroughly dealt with and when her eating-disordered behavior was under control. At that point, Mariko felt she could devote much of her energy to living her life instead of to her bulimia, as she had for so many years.

Phase Three: Reclaiming Life

Getting through the first two stages of treatment and recovery is a real achievement. As we've mentioned, during these two phases, your loved one has to spend considerable time and effort on her recovery. It can sometimes be difficult to have energy or time for anything else.

In the third and final phase of treatment, the focus shifts toward having a full life. Your loved one may have lost a great deal of time to her eating disorder, and she may feel as if a part of her life has passed her by. In this phase of treatment, she works to reclaim her life so she doesn't lose more of it to the disorder.

This final stage of treatment has three main interrelated goals. The first goal is maintenance of what she has accomplished in the previous two stages. This may mean, for instance, maintaining her weight in an appropriate range or relying on other ways of coping with her life than bingeing or purging. The second goal is to help her develop the kind of life that she wants for herself. This can mean resuming activities that she engaged in before the eating disorder interrupted her life, or it may mean pursuing new interests. The final goal of this phase is learning to be fully in her life without falling back into the eating disorder.

This phase of treatment has its own challenges. In the first two phases of treatment, your loved one has probably focused intently on her treatment and recovery. She may have taken time off from school or work, or she may have cut back on other activities so she has time for treatment. She also may have needed to change things (like the amount of time she spends exercising) to stabilize the eating disorder. People have told us that in the first two phases of treatment, it can feel like they are doing nothing else besides trying to recover.

As difficult and consuming as these first phases can be, they bring a kind of simplicity and clarity; the focus is on treatment and recovery. In the third phase of treatment, she is trying to balance many different things with her recovery. She may be going to school, working at a job, being a wife or mother, adding more exercise, or spending more time with friends. These can be wonderful, fulfilling activities, but they can complicate her effort to stay on track with her recovery. The challenge of this final stage of treatment is to achieve a healthy balance between everything she wants in her life.

The rewards of this phase are numerous. By this point, the eating disorder no longer consumes her every thought, and she has the freedom and peace of mind that was missing when the disorder was at its most intense. In addition, she is more able to accept herself as a valuable person and less likely to simply base her self-esteem on her body size. Furthermore, relationships with herself and with others have begun to take precedence over her relationship with the eating disorder.

In terms of treatment plans, the goal of this phase is to gradually decrease the frequency of her appointments as she feels ready. When and how to accomplish this is a matter for her and her treatment team to decide. There is no one right way to do it. The important thing for your loved one is to consistently feel that she is still getting the right amount of support.

Now we'll take a final look at Karen and Mariko and see how they handled this last phase of treatment.

Karen's Return to Life

Karen took off some time from college during her sophomore year. During the fall term, she simply wasn't strong enough to participate in school, and she spent most of that term in the eating-disorders program. She spent the spring term concentrating on her recovery. Karen returned to college that next fall. Her weight was stable, although she had not regained all the weight she needed to.

> *I felt ready to go back. I had worked really hard and had taken a lot of time off already, which was good. I can see now that I needed to do that, even though I had been SO afraid of what might happen if I left school. I still had some work to do, but it seemed like I was strong enough to deal with school.*

Returning to school was stressful for Karen. It was difficult to begin studying again and to get used to long days where she had several classes, and then homework. She missed her friends, but she also felt awkward about seeing them again.

> *I didn't really know what to tell them or how to talk to them about what I had been doing. My closest ones already knew, of course, since I had talked to them, even when I was in the hospital. Other people only knew that I had left school. I didn't know what to say.*

She also felt like she was behind her friends because she had missed an entire year. They were all juniors now, and she was still a sophomore.

> *I sort of thought I failed and disappointed my parents by taking time off. They kept telling me they were just glad that I was healthy enough to get back to my life. But I still worried. I worried about that with my friends too.... Did they think I was a loser? Were they disappointed in me for leaving school?*

As Karen became stronger, she wanted to decrease her treatment to have time for other things, such as school and friends. By the time she returned to school, she was healthy enough to go for medical check-ups only once a month. She had also decreased her therapy visits to one time each week. During the fall term, she decreased the appointments with the dietitian to every other week.

All these changes in treatment were adjustments for Karen. For each alteration in Karen's treatment plan, it took her several weeks to become completely accustomed to the new routine.

Each time we changed something, even when it was my idea and I wanted it, it was scary. I would worry about what would happen and if I was going to be okay. But I trusted that the team wouldn't let me do anything they thought I couldn't handle.

Karen sometimes had trouble balancing school and her recovery.

It was easy to skip meals when I had a class to go to or lots of studying to do. I had to pay close attention to eating enough, and that was annoying, but I knew I had to do it if I wanted to get through school in one piece.

It was also awkward for her when friends wanted to go out for dinner. She still didn't feel comfortable eating at many restaurants, but she didn't want to be conspicuous by telling her friends that she could only eat at certain places.

Sometimes they'd want to go somewhere that I knew there was nothing I could eat. I'd go anyway and just have a Diet Coke. It was too hard to tell them I couldn't find anything to eat there. I didn't want to be a bother, or to stand out.

In general, Karen's recovery was going very well.

I stumbled sometimes, but I think most people probably do. It helped to be reminded that I didn't have to be perfect at recovering from anorexia.

Karen was proud of herself and felt committed to her recovery. As she got used to being in school again, incorporating adequate nutrition became easier and easier. By the spring semester, she could go to most restaurants with her friends and could always find something she could order. Her weight continued to remain in a healthy range, and she was able to increase her exercise to the point it had been before she became ill.

The summer after her return to school, Karen got a job as a counselor at a summer camp about a hundred miles from home.

> *At first I worried about being away from home and about having to eat whatever the camp offered. At the same time, I wanted to do it. I thought I could handle most things that might happen there, and, if not, I could always come home.*

It did prove to be an adjustment to be at camp. However, Karen relied on everything she had learned about recovery and was able to stay healthy throughout the summer. Karen told us she found it "amazing that I could have such a good time, that I wasn't obsessing about food or weight hardly at all."

That next school year, Karen felt ready to leave treatment entirely.

> *I hadn't been in treatment all summer, and things had gone really well. I knew if I ever needed to, or just wanted to, I could always call my treatment team.*

During the next few years, Karen continued to do very well. The anorexia became less of a factor in her life, and she felt like she was developing a life that she wanted for herself. When she encountered a stressful event or period in her life, she sometimes felt the "pull of the anorexia calling me to come back, like it wanted to help me feel more secure."

In times like this, she paid extra attention to taking care of herself and to getting the support she needed.

> Sometimes talking to friends or family was just what I needed, and sometimes I thought it would be good to just to check in with my therapist about what was going on.

After completing her undergraduate degree, Karen went off to graduate school in a different state. She felt ready and eager to take on this new challenge.

Mariko's Return to Life

The third year of treatment was full of changes for Mariko. She got married, changed jobs, and moved. She continued her treatment and remained committed to her recovery. "I still had trouble sometimes dealing with my feelings without using bingeing and purging," but each time she accomplished this, she felt "very proud, and like it reinforced that I could do this."

Mariko was gradually able to decrease her bingeing and purging to once per week and then to every other week. "If I had a particularly stressful week, I might binge more frequently, but in general I could keep doing it less and less over time."

She continued to see her therapist weekly and the dietitian every other week. She only needed to see her physician once a month because her physical health was much better at this point.

A year after getting married, Mariko became pregnant.

> We had been trying for several months, and we were so excited that it had finally worked. Since I wanted it so much, I didn't think about that it might affect my bulimia. I was really surprised when that happened. I suddenly felt freaked out, like I was going to get fat, like I was out of control, and like my body was out to get me. I was terrified.

She began to binge and purge daily and felt "disgusted and disappointed" in herself.

Mariko saw her therapist, dietitian, and physician more frequently during this time. They worked together to help Mariko understand why being pregnant was making her so anxious and to help her reduce the bingeing and purging. "I could see how, despite truly wanting this baby, becoming pregnant had triggered some of those old feelings from having been attacked." She felt that "somehow I was infected or unclean, and that made me want to throw up." She also recognized that having a baby growing inside her made her feel out of her control, and she needed help to trust that her body knew what to do with respect to having a baby.

As Mariko understood these issues, her anxiety decreased and her need for the bingeing and purging decreased with it. During the months that she was pregnant, she again got the behavior under control and felt proud of herself.

The baby was born healthy, and Mariko went through another adjustment: being a mother. Mariko knew she needed support for fears of—as she told us—"whether I'd be a good enough mom, or whether I'd do something wrong." She realized she was afraid that she couldn't protect her child, just the way she couldn't protect herself when she had been 15.

She worked on these issues in therapy, and they became easier to deal with. Her husband also came to therapy with her sometimes so he could understand what she was going through and know best how to help her.

As the baby grew, Mariko "felt more confident in my ability to be a good mother. And as my confidence got better, I needed to binge and purge much less." As the baby turned 2, Mariko found herself bingeing and purging only once every five or six months—an enormous reduction from the three to five times per day she binged and purged when she began treatment.

At this point, Mariko felt she was in a place of maintenance in terms of her eating disorder. "I still hoped that there would be a point where I would never binge and purge again," and she intended to continue working toward that. But, she felt she was "really living my life" now, and that the eating disorder did not affect her at all like it had a few years back.

Conclusion

For many people, identifying these phases is very helpful. As we have said, treatment for an eating disorder can be complicated and sometimes long term. We have found that marking the passage of a phase can help an individual and her family see how much progress has actually occurred. It also helps them pace themselves and to anticipate what might happen next, so there will be fewer surprises along the way. The more information people have about how treatment and recovery work, the more secure and confident they usually feel about undertaking such a task.

Karen and Mariko each had their own path to recovery. From reading their stories, we can see how unique each of their lives were. We can also see the similarities in the meaning their eating disorders had for them. Both of them used the disorder to help them deal with emotions, with how they felt about themselves and their lives, and with their relationships.

8

How Can I Help?
The Support Network

○ ○
"I feel so powerless to do anything for her. All I want is to make things better, but I don't know what to do."

—*Comments from the husband of a 30-year-old woman with bulimia*

Over and over, parents, spouses, and other loved ones tell us they want to help, but they don't know what to do. You can't fix her eating disorder, because only she can do that, but you can do things that *are* very helpful and supportive. Don't underestimate the positive influence you can have.

What follows are some general guidelines of what you can do to help a loved one who is suffering from an eating disorder. These are only general guidelines. The best way to find out what your loved one finds helpful is to talk with her about it. She may not know right away, but if you keep asking, and she believes you truly want to know, she will eventually come up with some ideas.

Support

One factor that affects someone's recovery is the amount of support she has. In general, the more support, the better. Recovery can feel lonely and difficult at times, and having people around that she knows care about her makes a significant difference.

Listen

Listening can't be emphasized enough. As we have said earlier in the book, people who have eating disorders tend to feel deeply misunderstood and as if people do not care about what they are going through.

Simply being available to listen to her when she has something to tell you is perhaps the greatest gift you can offer. It may not always be easy. Sometimes she may say things that are hard to understand, that frighten you, or that even make you mad. But, if you consistently listen to her, she will feel that you care and that you want her around. This will be a help to her self-esteem and her desire to recover. Here are some things that people told us about listening:

> I never felt like anyone cared. Every time I tried to tell them something, they would have some advice, like, "Well, if you just stop throwing up, you'd feel a lot better." But all I really wanted was for them to just let me talk.

> I didn't need them to fix anything—I knew I had to do that myself—but they seemed to feel it was their responsibility to do something. What would have been the best is for them to ask how I was, what I was thinking, what was going on with me.

> I really wanted to just talk to them. I didn't even know what I wanted to say. I wanted them to hear me.

> My mom and dad finally sat me down and asked me what was happening, what I was doing to myself. It was really hard, but I told them, and they were great. They didn't make me feel like I was bad or gross. I could tell they wanted to help, to find out what I wanted.

Tell the Truth

Of course, you don't have to be silent when she talks to you. It's important that you communicate with her. Many times family and friends feel they have to "walk on egg shells" around their loved ones. They don't want to make things worse or to alienate her, so they don't say what they want to, but this just ends up making things worse. She usually can tell that you feel uncomfortable and afraid to say anything, and you will likely end up feeling resentful and somewhat restrained.

Telling her what you really think and feel is imperative, but, remember, the way in which you say something is very important. You'll want to be thoughtful and careful when you speak.

We have found that if you can speak in the first person (using statements that begin with, "I feel…" or "I'm worried about…" for example), your loved one will have the best chance of being able to hear you and to not feel threatened. For instance, you can say, "I'm concerned about you and worried about your health" instead of "You are killing yourself and I want you to stop right now." The point in both of these is similar, but the tone is less confrontational in the first, which makes it easier for your loved one to hear and to not become defensive.

Speaking in the first person can be difficult at times. Sometimes family and friends become so frightened or exhausted that they just feel like they're going to explode. At times like this, it can be very hard to think through what you want to say. Don't expect yourself to be perfect.

A mother of a teenager with anorexia told us, "I had so much I wanted to say to her. I was so afraid for her. I didn't want to scare her, though, or make things worse. So, I didn't ever say anything."

And the husband of someone with bulimia said, "It was frustrating. I wasn't sure what was okay to say and what wasn't. I didn't want to hurt her feelings, but I also didn't want to lie and pretend that I didn't have any feelings of my own about what was going on with her."

Your Emotions Are Normal

Being in a relationship with someone who has an eating disorder can be frightening, confusing, frustrating, and intense. This is normal. After all, your loved one is in a dangerous situation. Sometimes family and friends worry that what they are feeling isn't okay or think they should feel something else. Here are some things friends or family have told us.

> *I was angry at her. I mean, I couldn't understand why she was doing this to herself. It didn't make sense to me, and I couldn't see why she couldn't stop. Then I started feeling bad about being so angry. I mean, maybe I should have controlled myself better.*

> *Usually I can figure out my life. I am smart and have an education and a good job, but this eating disorder thing, it is simply beyond me. I have never been so confused or upset in my life. Baffled. And helpless, like I don't have any idea what to do.*

> *So many emotions came up in me, and in the rest of our family. We weren't sure if that was normal. We had no one to talk to about it. We all felt bad, like maybe we were betraying her by having our own feelings and reactions about her illness.*

> *My emotions were all over the place. One minute I wanted to scream. The next minute I wanted to cry. Then give up. Then hold her. It felt so crazy.*

Don't Let It Consume You Or Your Family

An eating disorder can consume not only the life of the person who has the disorder, but also her entire family and social group. It's not hard to see how this happens. After all, the eating disorder can be serious, and you don't want to ignore it. You want your loved one to know that you care and that you are trying to help her.

At the same time, anorexia or bulimia can become the focus to such a degree that your lives revolve around it. This actually isn't helpful for anyone. Consider the following comments from friends and family.

> *All we would talk about was the bulimia. It was like there wasn't anything else in our lives.*

I would feel so guilty, planning a party or going to a movie. Like we shouldn't do any of those things with her ill. Like our complete attention should be on her.

We would try to take her out, you know, go to the movies or whatever, but it was so awkward. No one knew what to say except about how was she doing and such. None of us could even think about anything else.

We used to have so much fun with her, but now she can only think about the disorder. And that makes us able to only think about it, too. It's scary.

Our house can feel as if someone died. It is always so serious, and it seems like everyone feels they can't have any fun, like it's against the law or something. Stupid anorexia! It has ruined everything.

Sometimes you need to do things together and talk about things that are completely unrelated to the disorder. Remember that there is life beyond the disorder. Also, by not exclusively focusing on the eating disorder, it will show your loved one that there is more to life than her disorder.

Just as importantly, it helps her see that you aren't becoming overwhelmed or taken in by the disorder—that you are able to maintain a life and help her create a life without the disease.

Take Care Of Yourself

This can't be stressed enough. Sometimes it can be difficult to remember to take care of yourself when your loved one is having such a hard time. But remember, in addition to being no good for yourself if you aren't doing well, you will be no good to her. Oftentimes, relatives or friends feel like they should devote all their attention, time, and energy to dealing with the illness. This may work in times of crisis or for very short periods of time, but it won't work for long.

You will need strength and patience to be able to be there for her as she recovers. If you aren't taking enough time for yourself, if you aren't having any fun, if you aren't making sure your other relationships are in good shape, and if you aren't paying attention to what you need and want, you won't be able to really be there for her.

As we have said, the person who has the disorder needs a strong support system. You do, too. People find various ways of getting the support they need. Friends and family can be of tremendous value. So can professionals. Sometimes you may be able to find a support group for families of someone with an eating disorder, for example. Or you can ask any member of your loved one's treatment team for ideas or recommendations.

Parents and other caretakers, in particular, often have difficulty remembering to take good care of themselves. Some told us:

I just felt I needed to be there for her all the time. It didn't matter what I felt like or what I wanted. I thought I had to give everything to her, but it ended up wearing me out.

I wanted to fix things so badly. I thought that if I tried harder and harder and worked harder and harder at it, she would get better faster. I gave up everything else I was doing—friends, entertaining, took time off from work, you name it—and you know what? It didn't even help. I mean, I know she was grateful that I tried, but she felt smothered and I felt exhausted and resentful.

I thought it meant I was a bad mom if I did anything for myself while she was ill. I thought it meant I didn't care.

Our daughter's therapist told us we had to do things for fun. I thought she was kidding. Who could have fun at a time like this? But she turned out to be right. It was hard at first. We worried that our daughter wouldn't be okay if we didn't watch her all the time. But we all adjusted. Now we do things for fun—by ourselves and also with our daughter, when she wants to join us.

I felt stupid getting help for myself. There wasn't anything wrong with me. It was my daughter who needed the help. Boy, was I wrong! I saw right away that I needed so much support and I had a lot of questions that I wanted answered—questions about what I should do, how I should act, what was okay—many, many questions. This gave me my own place I could go to talk about how my daughter's illness was affecting me and my wife. I think I'm a better parent to our daughter because of it. I understand more and can be there for her better.

Learn All You Can About Eating Disorders

Being educated about anorexia and bulimia gives you power. Based on your knowledge of what these disorders are and how to treat them, you can make the most educated decisions about how to proceed. In addition to this, your loved one will probably be grateful that you care enough to learn about her condition.

Be Patient

It is possible to recover from an eating disorder, but, as we have mentioned, it can take a while and be a complicated task. It is important to pace yourself so you don't get burned out. A young woman with bulimia told us,

> *I knew I could recover. Well, most of the time I knew it. I guess my family knew it also, because they never gave up. And I'm truly grateful. They kept hanging in there, even when it was tough. It took a long time, but I finally made it. We all did.*

APPENDIX
Helpful Resources

In this section, we have included some helpful resources. When you are calling around gathering information, do not be shy. Ask a lot of questions.

Fortunately, there are good resources out there to help your loved one. However, you may have to do some searching before you find the one that is right for your loved one. Be persistent and don't give up.

Helpful Organizations

Eating Disorder Referral and Information Center
(858) 792-7463 www.edreferral.com

Provides a list of treatment providers and facilities. In addition, provides information on a variety of topics related to eating disorders.

National Association of Anorexia Nervosa & Associated Disorders
(847) 831-3438

This organization provides a crisis hotline and maintains a list of providers and treatment facilities.

National Eating Disorder Association
(206) 382-3587 www.nationaleatingdisorders.org

This organization is dedicated to expanding public understanding of eating disorders and promoting access to treatment and support to family and loved ones.

Residential and Inpatient Treatment Programs

Here is a small sampling of treatment programs. Thoroughly research any program you may be considering for your loved one.

Center for Change Orem, Utah
(888) 224-8250 www.centerforchange.com

Center for Discovery Downey, California
(562) 882-1265 www.centerfordiscovery.com

Laureate Tulsa, Oklahoma
(800) 322-5173 www.laureate.com

Montecatini Carlsbad, California
(760) 436-8930 www.montecatinieatingdisorder.com

Monte Nido Malibu, California
(310) 457-9958 www.montenido.com

Oceanaire Redondo Beach, California
(310) 543-1010 www.oceanaireinc.com

Rader Institute Oxnard, California
(800) 841-1515 www.raderprograms.com

Remuda Ranch Wickenburg, Arizona
(800) 445-1900 www.remudaranch.com

Renfrew Center Pennsylvania, Florida, New York,
New Jersey, Connecticut
(800) 332-8415 www.renfrewcenter.com

Rosewood Ranch Wickenburg, Arizona
(800) 845-2211 www.rosewoodranch.com

Sutter Hospital Sacramento, California
(916) 386-3020 www.suttermedicalcenter.org

About the Authors

Tony Paulson, Ph.D.

Dr. Tony Paulson holds a bachelor's degree in psychology and a master's degree in social work, both from Sacramento State University. Following his years at Sacramento, he attended the Saybrook Institute, where he earned his doctorate. During his doctoral training, he received the Charles Thuss Award for exceptional writing and research, based on his work in eating disorders.

Dr. Paulson began treating people who were suffering from anorexia and bulimia nervosa more than 13 years ago. He quickly discovered a passion for this population, and a great desire to contribute in a meaningful way to the understanding of these disorders in an effort to alleviate the tremendous suffering these patients endure. Early in his career, he committed himself to compassionate, effective treatment, and to increasing patient and family understanding of what anorexia and bulimia are all about.

Dr. Paulson currently works as program director of an intensive outpatient program and an inpatient program serving Northern California. Over the past six years, he has developed and implemented treatment programs for people with eating disorders, given professional presentations on state and national levels, and frequently lectures to community groups throughout Northern California. He has conducted intensive in-depth research on eating disorders that has won praise from his colleagues.

Johanna Marie McShane, Ph.D.

Dr. Johanna Marie McShane has been working in the field of eating disorders treatment for thirteen years. She was staff therapist and assessment/intake counselor for the Serenity Eating Disorders Program at Mt. Diablo

Medical Pavilion, an inpatient eating disorders program in Northern California, from 1991 to 1994. She was a founding member and director of psychotherapies at the Integrated Therapies Program for Eating Disorders, an intensive outpatient program also in Northern California, from 1996 to 1998. Dr. McShane has been in private practice in Lafayette, California, for ten years, working with adolescents and adults who have eating disorders, and their families and significant others.

In addition to working directly with patients, Dr. McShane leads seminars for professionals and facilitates workshops for people who suffer from eating disorders and their families. She has spoken extensively about causes and treatment of anorexia, bulimia, and binge-eating disorders, and regularly provides consultation for clinics, hospitals, and private practitioners.

Dr. McShane holds bachelor's and master's degrees in music. In addition, she has earned a master's degree in clinical psychology from John F. Kennedy University, as well as a doctoral degree from Saybrook Institute. Along with writing, she has a strong commitment to research in the field of eating disorders. Her most recent research on dissociation in bulimia nervosa was nominated for an outstanding research award in 2004.

0-595-32061-9

Printed in the United States
21579LVS00005B/515